Steps to Christ

Ellen G. White

A Treasure Chest
of Encouragement

**ALL THE STEPS NEEDED FOR A DEEPER
DAILY WALK WITH CHRIST**

**ALL THE STEPS NEEDED TO REMAIN CLOSE
BY HIS SIDE IN COMING YEARS**

**THIS IS A BOOK YOU WILL KEEP WITH YOU
FOR YEARS TO COME**

Harvestime Books

HB–125
Steps to Christ
by Ellen G. White

  Plus three additional chapters:

   Origin of Evil (Great Controversy, chapter 29, by E.G.W.)

   Entering Upon a Deeper Worship (by the publisher)

   Helpful Bible Studies (by the publisher)

Published by Harvestime Books

Altamont, TN 37301 USA

Printed in the United States of America

Cover and Text Copyright © 2011

With the exception of the Bible, in the past 100 years there is hardly another book which has had as many translations, printings, and copies as Steps to Christ. It has been appreciated by millions around the world.

For God so loved the world, that
He gave His only begotten Son, that
whosoever believeth in Him should
not perish, but have everlasting life.
— John 3:16

This book: *This edition includes the complete original book. Nothing the author wrote has been omitted or changed, except that key points are in bold.*

Bracketed numbers on page tops: *These refer to the standardized paging in the original, cloth-cover edition.*

Additional copies: *For additional copies of this book at remarkably low prices in boxful quantities, write to Harvestime Books, Altamont, TN 37301. When you write, ask for a copy of our "Missionary Book Order Sheet," containing low-cost boxful prices of this and other books, such as Great Controversy, Ministry of Healing, Christ's Object Lessons, Bible Readings, etc. (See last page in this book for information on current lowest, boxful prices.)*

Contents

Encouragement when You Need It

God's Love for Man

Nature and revelation alike testify of God's love. Our Father in heaven is the source of life, of wisdom, and of joy. Look at the wonderful and beautiful things of nature. Think of their marvelous adaptation to the needs and happiness, not only of man, but of all living creatures. **The sunshine and the rain, that gladden and refresh the earth, the hills and seas and plains, all speak to us of the Creator's love. It is God who supplies the daily needs of all His creatures.** In the beautiful words of the psalmist: "The eyes of all wait upon Thee; and Thou givest them their meat in due season. Thou openest Thine hand, and satisfiest the desire of every living thing." Psalm 145:15-16.

God made man perfectly holy and happy; and the fair earth, as it came from the Creator's hand, bore no blight of decay or shadow of the curse. **It is transgression of God's law—the law of love—that has brought woe and death.** Yet even amid the suffering that results from sin, God's love is revealed. It is written that God cursed the ground for man's sake (Genesis 3:17). The thorn and the thistle—the difficulties and trials that make his life one of toil and care—were appointed for his good as a part of the training needful in God's plan for his uplifting from the ruin and degradation that sin has wrought. **The world, though fallen, is not all sorrow and misery. In nature itself are messages of hope and comfort.** There are flowers upon the thistles, and the thorns are covered with roses.

"God is love" is written upon every opening bud, upon every spire of springing grass. The lovely birds making the air vocal with their happy songs, the delicately tinted flowers in their perfection perfuming the air, the lofty trees of the forest with their rich foliage of living green—all testify to the tender, fatherly care of our God and to His desire to make His children happy.

The Word of God reveals His character. He Himself has declared His infinite love and pity. When Moses prayed, "Show me Thy glory," the Lord answered, "I will make all My goodness pass before thee" (Exodus 33:18-19). This is His glory. The Lord passed before Moses, and proclaimed, "The Lord, **The Lord God, merciful and gracious, long-suffering, and abundant in goodness and truth, keeping mercy for thousands, forgiving iniquity and transgression and sin."** Exodus 34:6-7. He is "slow to anger, and of great kindness" (Jonah 4:2) "because He delighteth in mercy" (Micah 7:18).

God has bound our hearts to Him by unnumbered tokens in heaven and in earth. **Through the things of nature, and the deepest and tenderest earthly ties that human hearts can know, He has sought to reveal Himself to us.** Yet these but imperfectly represent His love. Though all these evidences have been given, the enemy of good blinded the minds of men, so that they looked upon God with fear; they thought of Him as severe and unforgiving. **Satan led men to conceive of God as a being whose chief attribute is stern justice**,—one who is a severe judge, a harsh, exacting creditor. He pictured the Creator as a being who is watching with jealous eye to discern the errors and mistakes of men, that He may visit judgments upon them. **It was to remove this dark shadow, by revealing to the world the infinite love of God, that Jesus came to live among men.**

The Son of God came from heaven to make manifest the Father. "No man hath seen God at any time; the only begotten Son, which is in the bosom of the Father,

He hath declared Him." John 1:18. "Neither knoweth any man the Father, save the Son, and he to whomsoever the Son will reveal Him." Matthew 11:27. When one of the disciples made the request, "Show us the Father," Jesus answered, "Have I been so long time with you, and yet hast thou not known Me, Philip? He that hath seen Me hath seen the Father; and how sayest thou then, Show us the Father?" John 14:8-9.

In describing His earthly mission, **Jesus said, The Lord "hath anointed Me to preach the gospel to the poor; He hath sent Me to heal the brokenhearted, to preach deliverance to the captives**, and recovering of sight to the blind, to set at liberty them that are bruised." Luke 4:18. **This was His work. He went about doing good and healing all that were oppressed by Satan.** There were whole villages where there was not a moan of sickness in any house, for He had passed through them and healed all their sick. His work gave evidence of His divine anointing. **Love, mercy, and compassion were revealed in every act of His life; His heart went out in tender sympathy to the children of men.** He took man's nature, that He might reach man's wants. The poorest and humblest were not afraid to approach Him. Even little children were attracted to Him. They loved to climb upon His knees and gaze into the pensive face, benignant with love.

Jesus did not suppress one word of truth, but He uttered it always in love. He exercised the greatest tact and thoughtful, kind attention in His intercourse with the people. He was never rude, never needlessly spoke a severe word, never gave needless pain to a sensitive soul. He did not censure human weakness. **He spoke the truth, but always in love.** He denounced hypocrisy, unbelief, and iniquity; but tears were in His voice as He uttered His scathing rebukes. He wept over Jerusalem, the city He loved, which refused to receive Him, the way, the truth, and the life. They had rejected Him, the Saviour, but He regarded them with pitying tenderness. **His life was one of self-denial and thoughtful care for others. Every soul was precious in His eyes.** While He ever bore Himself with divine dignity, He bowed with the tenderest regard to every member of the family of God. **In all men He saw fallen souls whom it was His mission to save.**

Such is the character of Christ as revealed in His life. This is the character of God. It is from the Father's heart that the streams of divine compassion, manifest in Christ, flow out to the children of men. Jesus, the tender, pitying Saviour, was God "manifest in the flesh" (1 Timothy 3:16).

It was to redeem us that Jesus lived and suffered and died. He became "a Man of Sorrows," that we might be made partakers of everlasting joy. God permitted His beloved Son, full of grace and truth, to come from a world of indescribable glory, to a world marred and blighted with sin, darkened with the shadow of death and the curse. He permitted Him to leave the bosom of His love, the adoration of the angels, to suffer shame, insult, humiliation, hatred, and death. "The chastisement of our peace was upon Him; and with His stripes we are healed." Isaiah 53:5. **Behold Him in the wilderness, in Gethsemane, upon the cross! The spotless Son of God took upon Himself the burden of sin.** He who had been one with God, felt in His soul the awful separation that sin makes between God and man. This wrung from His lips the anguished cry, "My God, My God, why hast Thou forsaken Me?" Matthew 27:46. It was the burden of sin, the sense of its terrible enormity, of its separation of the soul from God—it was this that broke the heart of the Son of God.

But this great sacrifice was not made in order to create in the Father's heart a love for man, not to make Him willing to save. No, no! "God so loved the world, that He gave His only begotten Son." John 3:16. The Father loves us, not because of the great propitiation, but He provided the propitiation because He loves us. **Christ was the medium through which He could pour out His infinite love upon a fallen world. "God was in Christ, reconciling the world unto Himself."** 2 Corinthians 5:19. God suffered with His Son. In the agony of Gethsemane, the death of Calvary, the heart of Infinite Love paid the price of our redemption.

Jesus said, "Therefore doth My Father love Me, because I lay down My life, that I might take it again." John 10:17. That is, **"My Father has so loved you that He even loves Me more for giving My life to redeem you.** In becoming your Substitute and Surety, by surrendering My life, by taking your liabilities, your transgressions, I am endeared to My Father; for by My sacrifice, God can be just, and yet the Justifier of him who believeth in Jesus."

None but the Son of God could accomplish our redemption; for only He who was in the bosom of the Father could declare Him. Only He who knew the height and depth of the love of God could make it manifest. **Nothing less than the infinite sacrifice made by Christ in behalf of fallen man could express the Father's love to lost humanity.**

"God so loved the world, that He gave His only begotten Son." He gave Him not only to live among men, to bear their sins, and die their sacrifice. He gave Him to the fallen race. Christ was to identify Himself with the interests and needs of humanity. **He who was one with God has linked Himself with the children of men by ties that are never to be broken.** Jesus is "not ashamed to call them brethren" (Hebrews 2:11); He is our Sacrifice, our Advocate, our Brother, bearing our human form before the Father's throne, and through eternal ages one with the race He has redeemed—the Son of man. **And all this that man might be uplifted from the ruin and degradation of sin that he might reflect the love of God and share the joy of holiness.**

The price paid for our redemption, the infinite sacrifice of our heavenly Father in giving His Son to die for us, should give us exalted conceptions of what we may become through Christ. As the inspired apostle John beheld the height, the depth, the breadth of the Father's love toward the perishing race, he was filled with adoration and reverence; and, failing to find suitable language in which to express the greatness and tenderness of this love, he called upon the world to behold it. **"Behold, what manner of love the Father hath bestowed upon us, that we should be called the sons of God."** 1 John 3:1. What a value this places upon man! Through transgression the sons of man become subjects of Satan. **Through faith in the atoning sacrifice of Christ the sons of Adam may become the sons of God.** By assuming human nature, Christ elevates humanity. Fallen men are placed where, through connection with Christ, they may indeed become worthy of the name "sons of God."

Such love is without a parallel. Children of the heavenly King! Precious promise! Theme for the most profound meditation! **The matchless love of God for a world that did not love Him!** The thought has a subduing power upon the soul and brings the mind into captivity to the will of God. **The more we study the divine character in the light of the cross, the more we see mercy, tenderness, and forgiveness blended with equity and justice, and the more clearly we discern innumerable evidences of a love that is infinite** and a tender pity surpassing a mother's yearning sympathy for her wayward child.

The Sinner's Need of Christ

Man was originally endowed with noble powers and a well-balanced mind. He was perfect in his being, and in harmony with God. His thoughts were pure, his aims holy. **But through disobedience, his powers were perverted, and selfishness took the place of love.** His nature became so weakened through transgression that it was impossible for him, in his own strength, to resist the power of evil. **He was made captive by Satan, and would have remained so forever had not God specially interposed.** It was the tempter's purpose to thwart the divine plan in man's creation, and fill the earth with woe and desolation. And he would point to all this evil as the result of God's work in creating man.

In his sinless state, man held joyful communion with Him "in whom are hid all the treasures of wisdom and knowledge" (Colossians 2:3). But **after his sin, he could no longer find joy in holiness, and he sought to hide from the presence of God. Such is still the condition of the unrenewed heart.** It is not in harmony with God, and finds no joy in communion with Him. **The sinner could not be happy in God's presence; he would shrink from the companionship of holy beings.** Could he be permitted to enter heaven, it would have no joy for him. The spirit of unselfish love that reigns there—every heart responding to the heart of Infinite Love—would touch no answering chord in his soul. His thoughts, his interests, his motives, would be alien to those that actuate the sinless dwellers there. He would be a discordant note in the melody of heaven. Heaven would be to him a place of torture; he would long to be hidden from Him who is its light, and the center of its joy. **It is no arbitrary decree on the part of God that excludes the wicked from heaven; they are shut out by their own unfitness for its companionship.** The glory of God would be to them a consuming fire. They would welcome destruction, that they might be hidden from the face of Him who died to redeem them.

It is impossible for us, of ourselves, to escape from the pit of sin in which we are sunken. Our hearts are evil, and we cannot change them. "Who can bring a clean thing out of an unclean? not one." Job 14:4. "The carnal mind is enmity against God: for it is not subject to the law of God, neither indeed can be." Romans 8:7. Education, culture, the exercise of the will, human effort, all have their proper sphere, but here they are powerless. They may produce an outward correctness of behavior, but they cannot change the heart; they cannot purify the springs of life. **There must be a power working from within, a new life from above, before men can be changed from sin to holiness. That power is Christ.** His grace alone can quicken the lifeless faculties of the soul, and attract it to God, to holiness.

The Saviour said, "Except a man be born from above," unless he shall receive a new heart, new desires, purposes, and motives, leading to a new life, "he cannot see the kingdom of God" (John 3:3, margin). The idea that it is necessary only to develop the good that exists in man, by nature, is a fatal deception. "The natural man receiveth not the things of the Spirit of God: for they are foolishness unto him: neither can he know them, because they are spiritually discerned." 1 Corinthians 2:14. "Marvel not that I said unto thee, Ye must be born again." John 3:7. Of Christ it is written,

"In Him was life; and the life was the light of men" ..
there is no other "name under heaven given among
men, whereby we must be saved" (John 1:4; Acts 4:12).

It is not enough to perceive the loving-kindness
of God, to see the benevolence, the fatherly tenderness, of His character. It is not enough to discern the
wisdom and justice of His law, to see that it is founded
upon the eternal principle of love. Paul, the apostle, saw
all this when he exclaimed, "I consent unto the law that
it is good .. The law is holy, and the commandment holy,
and just, and good." But he added, in the bitterness of
his soul anguish and despair, "I am carnal, sold under
sin" (Romans 7:16, 12, 14). He longed for the purity,
the righteousness, to which in himself he was powerless to attain, and cried out, "O wretched man that I am!
who shall deliver me from this body of death?" Romans
7:24, margin. Such is the cry that has gone up from
burdened hearts in all lands and in all ages. To all,
there is but one answer, "Behold the Lamb of God,
which taketh away the sin of the world." John 1:29.

Many are the figures by which the Spirit of God has
sought to illustrate this truth, and make it plain to souls
that long to be freed from the burden of guilt. When,
after his sin in deceiving Esau, Jacob fled from his father's
home, he was weighed down with a sense of guilt. Lonely
and outcast as he was, separated from all that had made
life dear, the one thought that above all others pressed
upon his soul was the fear that his sin had cut him off
from God, that he was forsaken of Heaven. In sadness
he lay down to rest on the bare earth, around him only
the lonely hills, and above, the heavens bright with stars.
As he slept, a strange light broke upon his vision; and
lo, from the plain on which he lay, vast shadowy stairs
seemed to lead upward to the very gates of heaven,
and upon them angels of God were passing up and

down; while from the glory above, the divine voice was heard in a message of comfort and hope. Thus was made known to Jacob that which met the need and longing of his soul—a Saviour. **With joy and gratitude he saw revealed a way by which he, a sinner, could be restored to communion with God. The mystic ladder of his dream represented Jesus**, the only medium of communication between God and man.

This is the same figure to which Christ referred in His conversation with Nathanael, when He said, "Ye shall see heaven open, and the angels of God ascending and descending upon the Son of man" (John 1:51). **In the apostasy, man alienated himself from God; earth was cut off from heaven. Across the gulf that lay between, there could be no communion. But through Christ, earth is again linked with heaven.** With His own merits, Christ has bridged the gulf which sin had made, so that the ministering angels can hold communion with man. **Christ connects fallen man in his weakness and helplessness with the Source of infinite power.**

But in vain are men's dreams of progress, in vain all efforts for the uplifting of humanity, if they neglect the one Source of hope and help for the fallen race. "Every good gift and every perfect gift" (James 1:17) is from God. **There is no true excellence of character apart from Him. And the only way to God is Christ.** He says, "I am the way, the truth, and the life: no man cometh unto the Father, but by Me." John 14:6.

The heart of God yearns over His earthly children with a love stronger than death. In giving up His Son, He has poured out to us all heaven in one gift. The Saviour's life and death and intercession, the ministry of angels, the pleading of the Spirit, the Father working above and through all, the unceasing interest of heavenly beings,—all are enlisted in behalf of man's redemption.

Oh, let us contemplate the amazing sacrifice that has been made for us! **Let us try to appreciate the labor and energy that Heaven is expending to reclaim the lost, and bring them back to the Father's house.** Motives stronger, and agencies more powerful, could never be brought into operation; **the exceeding rewards for rightdoing, the enjoyment of heaven, the society of the angels, the communion and love of God and His Son, the elevation and extension of all our powers throughout eternal ages—are these not mighty incentives** and encouragements to urge us to give the heart's loving service to our Creator and Redeemer?

And, on the other hand, the judgments of God pronounced against sin, the inevitable retribution, the degradation of our character, and the final destruction are presented in God's Word to warn us against the service of Satan.

Shall we not regard the mercy of God? What more could He do? Let us place ourselves in right relation to Him who has loved us with amazing love. Let us avail ourselves of the means provided for us that we may be transformed into His likeness, and be restored to fellowship with the ministering angels, to harmony and communion with the Father and the Son.

Repentance

How shall a man be just with God? How shall the sinner be made righteous? It is only through Christ that we can be brought into harmony with God, with holiness; but how are we to come to Christ? Many are asking the same question as did the multitude on the Day of Pentecost, when, convicted of sin, **they cried out,**

"What shall we do?" The first word of Peter's answer was, "Repent." Acts 2:37-38. At another time, shortly after, he said, "Repent . . and be converted, that your sins may be blotted out." Acts 3:19.

Repentance includes sorrow for sin and a turning away from it. We shall not renounce sin unless we see its sinfulness; until we turn away from it in heart, there will be no real change in the life.

There are many who fail to understand the true nature of repentance. **Multitudes sorrow that they have sinned and even make an outward reformation because they fear that their wrongdoing will bring suffering upon themselves. But this is not repentance in the Bible sense. They lament the suffering rather than the sin.** Such was the grief of Esau when he saw that the birthright was lost to him forever. Balaam, terrified by the angel standing in his pathway with drawn sword, acknowledged his guilt lest he should lose his life; but **there was no genuine repentance for sin, no conversion of purpose, no abhorrence of evil**. Judas Iscariot, after betraying his Lord, exclaimed, "I have sinned in that I have betrayed the innocent blood." Matthew 27:4.

The confession was forced from his guilty soul by an awful sense of condemnation and a fearful looking for of judgment. **The consequences that were to result to him filled him with terror, but there was no deep, heartbreaking grief in his soul, that he had betrayed the spotless Son of God** and denied the Holy One of Israel. Pharaoh, when suffering under the judgments of God, acknowledged his sin in order to escape further punishment, but returned to his defiance of Heaven as soon as the plagues were stayed. **These all lamented the results of sin, but did not sorrow for the sin itself.**

But when the heart yields to the influence of the Spirit of God, the conscience will be quickened, and

the sinner will discern something of the depth and sacredness of God's holy law, the foundation of His government in heaven and on earth. The "Light, which lighteth every man that cometh into the world" (John 1:9), illumines the secret chambers of the soul, and the hidden things of darkness are made manifest. **Conviction takes hold upon the mind and heart.** The sinner has a sense of the righteousness of Jehovah and feels the terror of appearing, in his own guilt and uncleanness, before the Searcher of hearts. **He sees the love of God, the beauty of holiness, the joy of purity; he longs to be cleansed and to be restored to communion with Heaven.**

The prayer of David, after his fall, illustrates the nature of true sorrow for sin. **His repentance was sincere and deep. There was no effort to palliate his guilt; no desire to escape the judgment threatened inspired his prayer.** David saw the enormity of his transgression; he saw the defilement of his soul; he loathed his sin. **It was not for pardon only that he prayed, but for purity of heart. He longed for the joy of holiness—to be restored to harmony and communion with God.** This was the language of his soul.

"Blessed is he whose transgression is forgiven, whose sin is covered. Blessed is the man unto whom the Lord imputeth not iniquity, and in whose spirit there is no guile." Psalm 32:1-2. **"Have mercy upon me, O God, according to Thy loving-kindness**: According unto the multitude of Thy tender mercies blot out my transgressions . . For I acknowledge my transgressions: and my sin is ever before me . . **Purge me with hyssop, and I shall be clean: wash me, and I shall be whiter than snow . . Create in me a clean heart, O God; and renew a right spirit within me. Cast me not away from Thy presence**; and take not Thy Holy Spirit from me. Restore unto me the joy of Thy salvation; and uphold me with Thy free spirit . . Deliver me from bloodguiltiness, O God, Thou God of my salvation: And my tongue shall sing aloud of Thy righteousness." Psalm 51:1, 3, 7, 10-12, 14.

A repentance such as this is beyond the reach of our own power to accomplish; it is obtained only from Christ, who ascended up on high and has given gifts unto men.

Just here is a point on which many may err, and hence they fail of receiving the help that Christ desires to give them. **They think that they cannot come to Christ unless they first repent**, and that repentance prepares for the forgiveness of their sins. It is true that repentance does precede the forgiveness of sins; for **it is only the broken and contrite heart that will feel the need of a Saviour. But must the sinner wait till he has repented before he can come to Jesus?** Is repentance to be made an obstacle between the sinner and the Saviour?

The Bible does not teach that the sinner must repent before he can heed the invitation of Christ, "Come unto Me, all ye that labor and are heavy laden, and I will give you rest." Matthew 11:28. It is the virtue that goes forth from Christ, that leads to genuine repentance. Peter made the matter clear in his statement to the Israelites when he said, "Him hath God exalted with His right hand to be a Prince and a Saviour, for to give repentance to Israel, and forgiveness of sins." Acts 5:31. **We can no more repent without the Spirit of Christ to awaken the conscience than we can be pardoned without Christ.**

Christ is the source of every right impulse. He is the only one that can implant in the heart enmity against sin. Every desire for truth and purity, every conviction of our own sinfulness, is an evidence that His Spirit is moving upon our hearts.

Jesus has said, "I, if I be lifted up from the earth,

will draw all men unto Me." John 12:32. **Christ must be revealed to the sinner as the Saviour dying for the sins of the world; and as we behold the Lamb of God upon the cross of Calvary, the mystery of redemption begins to unfold to our minds, and the goodness of God leads us to repentance.** In dying for sinners, Christ manifested a love that is incomprehensible; and as the sinner beholds this love, it softens the heart, impresses the mind, and inspires contrition in the soul.

It is true that men sometimes become ashamed of their sinful ways, and give up some of their evil habits, before they are conscious that they are being drawn to Christ. But **whenever they make an effort to reform, from a sincere desire to do right, it is the power of Christ that is drawing them.** An influence of which they are unconscious works upon the soul, and the conscience is quickened, and the outward life is amended. **And as Christ draws them to look upon His cross, to behold Him whom their sins have pierced, the commandment comes home to the conscience. The wickedness of their life, the deep-seated sin of the soul, is revealed to them.** They begin to comprehend something of the righteousness of Christ, and exclaim, **"What is sin, that it should require such a sacrifice for the redemption of its victim?** Was all this love, all this suffering, all this humiliation, demanded, that we might not perish, but have everlasting life?"

The sinner may resist this love, may refuse to be drawn to Christ; but if he does not resist he will be drawn to Jesus; a knowledge of the plan of salvation will lead him to the foot of the cross in repentance for his sins, which have caused the sufferings of God's dear Son.

The same divine mind that is working upon the things of nature is speaking to the hearts of men and

creating an inexpressible craving for something they have not. The things of the world cannot satisfy their longing. **The Spirit of God is pleading with them to seek for those things that alone can give peace and rest—the grace of Christ, the joy of holiness.** Through influences seen and unseen, our Saviour is constantly at work to attract the minds of men from the unsatisfying pleasures of sin to the infinite blessings that may be theirs in Him. To all these souls, who are vainly seeking to drink from the broken cisterns of this world, the divine message is addressed, "Let him that is athirst come. And whosoever will, let him take the water of life freely." Revelation 22:17.

You who in heart long for something better than this world can give, recognize this longing as the voice of God to your soul. Ask Him to give you repentance, to reveal Christ to you in His infinite love, in His perfect purity. In the Saviour's life the principles of God's law—love to God and man—were perfectly exemplified. Benevolence, unselfish love, was the life of His soul. It is as we behold Him, as the light from our Saviour falls upon us, that we see the sinfulness of our own hearts.

We may have flattered ourselves, as did Nicodemus, that our life has been upright, that our moral character is correct, and think that we need not humble the heart before God, like the common sinner; but, when the light from Christ shines into our souls, we shall see how impure we are; we shall discern the selfishness of motive, the enmity against God, that has defiled every act of life. Then we shall know that our own righteousness is indeed as filthy rags, and that the blood of Christ alone can cleanse us from the defilement of sin, and renew our hearts in His own likeness.

One ray of the glory of God, one gleam of the purity of Christ, penetrating the soul, makes every spot

**of defilement painfully distinct, and lays bare the de-
formity and defects of the human character.** It makes
apparent the unhallowed desires, the infidelity of the
heart, the impurity of the lips. The sinner's acts of disloyalty, in making void the law of God, are exposed to his
sight, and his spirit is stricken and afflicted under the
searching influence of the Spirit of God. He loathes himself as he views the pure, spotless character of Christ.

When the prophet, Daniel, beheld the glory surrounding the heavenly messenger that was sent unto him, he
was overwhelmed with a sense of his own weakness and
imperfection. Describing the effect of the wonderful scene,
he says, "There remained no strength in me: for my come-
liness was turned in me into corruption, and I retained
no strength." Daniel 10:8. **The soul thus touched will
hate its selfishness, abhor its self-love, and will seek,
through Christ's righteousness, for the purity of heart
that is in harmony with the law of God and the character of Christ.**

Paul says that as "touching the righteousness which
is in the law"—as far as outward acts were concerned—
he was "blameless" (Philippians 3:6); but when the spiritual character of the law was discerned, he saw himself
a sinner. **Judged by the letter of the law as men apply
it to the outward life, he had abstained from sin; but
when he looked into the depths of its holy precepts,
and saw himself as God saw him, he bowed in humiliation and confessed his guilt.** He says, "I was alive without the law once: but when the commandment came, sin
revived, and I died." Romans 7:9. When he saw the spiritual nature of the law, sin appeared in its true hideous-
ness, and his self-esteem was gone.

God does not regard all sins as of equal magnitude;
there are degrees of guilt in His estimation, as well as in
that of man's; but **however trifling this or that wrong**

act may seem in the eyes of men, no sin is small in the sight of God. Man's judgment is partial, imperfect; but God estimates all things as they really are. The drunkard is despised and is told that his sin will exclude him from heaven while pride, selfishness, and covetousness too often go unrebuked. But these are sins that are especially offensive to God; for they are contrary to the benevolence of His character, to that unselfish love which is the very atmosphere of the unfallen universe. He who falls into some of the grosser sins may feel a sense of his shame and poverty and his need of the grace of Christ; but **pride feels no need, and so it closes the heart against Christ and the infinite blessings He came to give.**

The poor publican who prayed, "God be merciful to me a sinner" (Luke 18:13), regarded himself as a very wicked man, and others looked upon him in the same light; but he felt his need, and with his burden of guilt and shame he came before God, asking for His mercy. His heart was open for the Spirit of God to do its gracious work and set him free from the power of sin. The Pharisee's boastful, self-righteous prayer showed that his heart was closed against the influence of the Holy Spirit. Because of his distance from God, he had no sense of his own defilement, in contrast with the perfection of the divine holiness. He felt no need, and he received nothing.

If you see your sinfulness, do not wait to make yourself better. How many there are who think they are not good enough to come to Christ. Do you expect to become better through your own efforts? "Can the Ethiopian change his skin, or the leopard his spots? then may ye also do good, that are accustomed to do evil." Jeremiah 13:23. **There is help for us only in God. We must not wait for stronger persuasions, for better opportunities, or for holier tempers. We can do noth-**

ing of ourselves. We must come to Christ just as we are.

But let none deceive themselves with the thought that God, in His great love and mercy, will yet save even the rejecters of His grace. **The exceeding sinfulness of sin can be estimated only in the light of the cross. When men urge that God is too good to cast off the sinner, let them look to Calvary.** It was because there was no other way in which man could be saved, because without this sacrifice it was impossible for the human race to escape from the defiling power of sin, and be restored to communion with holy beings,—impossible for them again to become partakers of spiritual life,—it was because of this that Christ took upon Himself the guilt of the disobedient and suffered in the sinner's stead. **The love and suffering and death of the Son of God all testify to the terrible enormity of sin and declare that there is no escape from its power, no hope of the higher life, but through the submission of the soul to Christ.**

The impenitent sometimes excuse themselves by saying of professed Christians, "I am as good as they are. They are no more self-denying, sober, or circumspect in their conduct than I am. They love pleasure and self-indulgence as well as I do." Thus they make the faults of others an excuse for their own neglect of duty. **But the sins and defects of others do not excuse anyone, for the Lord has not given us an erring human pattern. The spotless Son of God has been given as our example**, and those who complain of the wrong course of professed Christians are the ones who should show better lives and nobler examples. If they have so high a conception of what a Christian should be, is not their own sin so much the greater? They know what is right, and yet refuse to do it.

Beware of procrastination. Do not put off the work

of forsaking your sins and seeking purity of heart through Jesus. Here is where thousands upon thousands have erred to their eternal loss. I will not here dwell upon the shortness and uncertainty of life; but there is a terrible danger—a danger not sufficiently understood—in delaying to yield to the pleading voice of God's Holy Spirit, in choosing to live in sin; for such this delay really is. **Sin, however small it may be esteemed, can be indulged in only at the peril of infinite loss. What we do not overcome will overcome us and work out our destruction.**

Adam and Eve persuaded themselves that, in so small a matter as eating of the forbidden fruit, there could not result such terrible consequences as God had declared. **But this small matter was the transgression of God's immutable and holy law, and it separated man from God and opened the floodgates of death and untold woe upon our world.** Age after age, there has gone up from our earth a continual cry of mourning, and the whole creation groaneth and travaileth together in pain as a consequence of man's disobedience. **Heaven itself has felt the effects of his rebellion against God. Calvary stands as a memorial of the amazing sacrifice required to atone for the transgression of the divine law. Let us not regard sin as a trivial thing.**

Every act of transgression, every neglect or rejection of the grace of Christ is reacting upon yourself; it is hardening the heart, depraving the will, benumbing the understanding, and not only making you less inclined to yield, but less capable of yielding to the tender pleading of God's Holy Spirit.

Many are quieting a troubled conscience with the thought that they can change a course of evil when they choose; that they can trifle with the invitations of mercy, and yet be again and again impressed. They think that after doing despite to the Spirit of grace, after casting their influence on the side of Satan, in a moment of terrible extremity they can change their course. But this is not so easily done. The experience, the education, of a lifetime, has so thoroughly molded the character that few then desire to receive the image of Jesus.

Even one wrong trait of character, one sinful desire, persistently cherished, will eventually neutralize all the power of the gospel. Every sinful indulgence strengthens the soul's aversion to God. The man who manifests an infidel hardihood or a stolid indifference to divine truth is but reaping the harvest of that which he has himself sown. In all the Bible there is not a more fearful warning against trifling with evil than the words of the wise man that the sinner "shall be holden with the cords of his sins" (Proverbs 5:22).

Christ is ready to set us free from sin, but He does not force the will; and if, by persistent transgression, the will itself is wholly bent on evil, and we do not *desire* to be set free, if we *will* not accept His grace, what more can He do? We have destroyed ourselves by our determined rejection of His love. "Behold, now is the accepted time; behold, now is the day of salvation." 2 Corinthians 6:2. "Today if ye will hear His voice, harden not your hearts." Hebrews 3:7-8.

"Man looketh on the outward appearance, but the Lord looketh on the heart" (1 Samuel 16:7)—the human heart, with its conflicting emotions of joy and sorrow; the wandering, wayward heart, which is the abode of so much impurity and deceit. He knows its motives, its very intents and purposes. **Go to Him with your soul all stained as it is.** Like the psalmist, **throw its chambers open to the all-seeing eye**, exclaiming, "Search me, O God, and know my heart: try me, and know my thoughts: and see if there be any wicked way in me, and lead me in the way everlasting." Psalm 139:23-24.

Many accept an intellectual religion, a form of godliness, when the heart is not cleansed. Let it be your prayer, "Create in me a clean heart, O God; and renew a right spirit within me." Psalm 51:10. **Deal truly with your own soul. Be as earnest, as persistent, as you would be if your mortal life were at stake. This is a matter to be settled between God and your own soul, settled for eternity**. A supposed hope, and nothing more, will prove your ruin.

Study God's Word prayerfully. That Word presents before you, in the law of God and the life of Christ, the great principles of holiness, without which "no man shall see the Lord." Hebrews 12:14. It convinces of sin; it plainly reveals the way of salvation. Give heed to it as the voice of God speaking to your soul.

As you see the enormity of sin, as you see yourself as you really are, do not give up to despair. It was sinners that Christ came to save. We have not to reconcile God to us, but—O wondrous love!—God in Christ is "reconciling the world unto Himself" (2 Corinthians 5:19). He is wooing by His tender love the hearts of His erring children. No earthly parent could be as patient with the faults and mistakes of his children, as is God with those He seeks to save. No one could plead more tenderly with the transgressor. No human lips ever poured out more tender entreaties to the wanderer than does He. All His promises, His warnings, are but the breathing of unutterable love.

When Satan comes to tell you that you are a great sinner, look up to your Redeemer and talk of His merits. That which will help you is to look to His light. **Acknowledge your sin, but tell the enemy that "Christ Jesus came into the world to save sinners" and that you may be saved by His matchless love** (1 Timothy

1:15). Jesus asked Simon a question in regard to two debtors. One owed his lord a small sum, and the other owed him a very large sum; but he forgave them both, and Christ asked Simon which debtor would love his lord most. Simon answered, "He to whom he forgave most" (Luke 7:43). We have been great sinners, but Christ died that we might be forgiven. The merits of His sacrifice are sufficient to present to the Father in our behalf. **Those to whom He has forgiven most will love Him most, and will stand nearest to His throne to praise Him for His great love and infinite sacrifice. It is when we most fully comprehend the love of God that we best realize the sinfulness of sin.** When we see the length of the chain that was let down for us, when we understand something of the infinite sacrifice that Christ has made in our behalf, the heart is melted with tenderness and contrition.

Confession

"He that covereth his sins shall not prosper: but whoso confesseth and forsaketh them shall have mercy." Proverbs 28:13.

The conditions of obtaining the mercy of God are simple and just and reasonable. The Lord does not require us to do some grievous thing in order that we may have the forgiveness of sin. We need not make long and wearisome pilgrimages or perform painful penances to commend our souls to the God of heaven or to expiate our transgression; but he that confesseth and forsaketh his sin shall have mercy.

The apostle says, "Confess your faults one to another, and pray one for another, that ye may be healed."

James 5:16. **Confess your sins to God, who only can forgive them, and your faults to one another. If you have given offense to your friend or neighbor, you are to acknowledge your wrong, and it is his duty freely to forgive you.** Then you are to seek the forgiveness of God, because the brother you have wounded is the property of God, and in injuring him you sinned against his Creator and Redeemer. The case is brought before the only true Mediator, our great High Priest, who "was in all points tempted like as we are, yet without sin," and who is "touched with the feeling of our infirmities" (Hebrews 4:15), and is able to cleanse from every stain of iniquity.

Those who have not humbled their souls before God in acknowledging their guilt, have not yet fulfilled the first condition of acceptance. If we have not experienced that repentance which is not to be repented of, and have not with true humiliation of soul and brokenness of spirit confessed our sins, abhorring our iniquity, we have never truly sought for the forgiveness of sin; and if we have never sought, we have never found the peace of God. **The only reason why we do not have remission of sins that are past is that we are not willing to humble our hearts and comply with the conditions of the Word of truth.** Explicit instruction is given concerning this matter. **Confession of sin, whether public or private, should be heartfelt and freely expressed.** It is not to be urged from the sinner. It is not to be made in a flippant and careless way, or forced from those who have no realizing sense of the abhorrent character of sin. **The confession that is the outpouring of the inmost soul finds its way to the God of infinite pity.** The psalmist says, "The Lord is nigh unto them that are of a broken heart; and saveth such as be of a contrite spirit." Psalm 34:18.

True confession is always of a specific character,

and acknowledges particular sins. They may be of such a nature as to be brought before God only; they may be wrongs that should be confessed to individuals who have suffered injury through them; or they may be of a public character, and should then be as publicly confessed. **But all confession should be definite and to the point, acknowledging the very sins of which you are guilty.**

In the days of Samuel the Israelites wandered from God. They were suffering the consequences of sin; for they had lost their faith in God, lost their discernment of His power and wisdom to rule the nation, lost their confidence in His ability to defend and vindicate His cause. They turned from the great Ruler of the universe and desired to be governed as were the nations around them. Before they found peace they made this definite confession: "We have added unto all our sins this evil, to ask us a king." 1 Samuel 12:19. **The very sin of which they were convicted had to be confessed.** Their ingratitude oppressed their souls and severed them from God.

Confession will not be acceptable to God without sincere repentance and reformation. There must be decided changes in the life; everything offensive to God must be put away. This will be the result of genuine sorrow for sin. The work that we have to do on our part is plainly set before us: "Wash you, make you clean; put away the evil of your doings from before Mine eyes; cease to do evil; learn to do well; seek judgment, relieve the oppressed, judge the fatherless, plead for the widow." Isaiah 1:16-17. **"If the wicked restore the pledge, give again that he had robbed, walk in the statutes of life, without committing iniquity; he shall surely live, he shall not die."** Ezekiel 33:15. Paul says, speaking of the work of repentance: "Ye sorrowed after a godly sort, what carefulness it wrought in you, yea, what clearing of yourselves, yea, what indignation, yea, what fear, yea, what vehement desire, yea, what zeal, yea, what revenge! In all things ye have approved yourselves to be clear in this matter." 2 Corinthians 7:11.

When sin has deadened the moral perceptions, the wrongdoer does not discern the defects of his character nor realize the enormity of the evil he has committed; and, unless he yields to the convicting power of the Holy Spirit, he remains in partial blindness to his sin. His confessions are not sincere and in earnest. To every acknowledgment of his guilt he adds an apology in excuse of his course, declaring that if it had not been for certain circumstances he would not have done this or that for which he is reproved.

After Adam and Eve had eaten of the forbidden fruit, they were filled with a sense of shame and terror. **At first their only thought was how to excuse their sin and escape the dreaded sentence of death.** When the Lord inquired concerning their sin, Adam replied, laying the guilt partly upon God and partly upon his companion: "The woman whom Thou gavest to be with me, she gave me of the tree, and I did eat." The woman put the blame upon the serpent, saying, "The serpent beguiled me, and I did eat." Genesis 3:12-13. Why did You make the serpent? Why did You suffer him to come into Eden? **These were the questions implied in her excuse for her sin, thus charging God with the responsibility of their fall. The spirit of self-justification originated in the father of lies** and has been exhibited by all the sons and daughters of Adam. Confessions of this order are not inspired by the divine Spirit and will not be acceptable to God. **True repentance will lead a man to bear his guilt himself and acknowledge it without deception or hypocrisy.** Like the poor publican, not lifting up so much as his eyes unto heaven, he will cry, "God be merciful to me a sinner" and **those who do acknowl-**

edge their guilt will be justified, for Jesus will plead His blood in behalf of the repentant soul.

The examples in God's Word of genuine repentance and humiliation reveal a spirit of confession in which there is no excuse for sin or attempt at self-justification. Paul did not seek to shield himself; he paints his sin in its darkest hue, not attempting to lessen his guilt. He says, "Many of the saints did I shut up in prison, having received authority from the chief priests; and when they were put to death, I gave my voice against them. And I punished them oft in every synagogue, and compelled them to blaspheme; and being exceedingly mad against them, I persecuted them even unto strange cities." Acts 26:10-11. He does not hesitate to declare that "Christ Jesus came into the world to save sinners; of whom I am chief" (1 Timothy 1:15).

The humble and broken heart, subdued by genuine repentance, will appreciate something of the love of God and the cost of Calvary; and as a son confesses to a loving father, so will the truly penitent bring all his sins before God. And it is written, "If we confess our sins, He is faithful and just to forgive us our sins, and to cleanse us from all unrighteousness." 1 John 1:9.

Consecration

God's promise is, "Ye shall seek Me, and find Me, when ye shall search for Me with all your heart." Jeremiah 29:13.

The whole heart must be yielded to God or the change can never be wrought in us by which we are to be restored to His likeness. By nature we are alienated from God. The Holy Spirit describes our condition in such words as these: "Dead in trespasses and sins" (Ephesians 2:1), "the whole head is sick, and the whole heart faint . . no soundness in it" (Isaiah 1:5-6). We are held fast in the snare of Satan, "taken captive by him at his will" (2 Timothy 2:26). **God desires to heal us, to set us free. But since this requires an entire transformation, a renewing of our whole nature, we must yield ourselves wholly to Him.**

The warfare against self is the greatest battle that was ever fought. **The yielding of self, surrendering all to the will of God, requires a struggle; but the soul must submit to God before it can be renewed in holiness.**

The government of God is not, as Satan would make it appear, founded upon a blind submission, an unreasoning control. It appeals to the intellect and the conscience. "Come now, and let us reason together" (Isaiah 1:18) is the Creator's invitation to the beings He has made. **God does not force the will of His creatures. He cannot accept a homage that is not willingly and intelligently given.** A mere forced submission would prevent all real development of mind or character; it would make man a mere automaton. Such is not the purpose of the Creator. **He desires that man, the crowning work of His creative power, shall reach the highest possible development. He sets before us the height of blessing to which He desires to bring us through His grace. He invites us to give ourselves to Him, that He may work His will in us.** It remains for us to choose whether we will be set free from the bondage of sin, to share the glorious liberty of the sons of God.

In giving ourselves to God, we must necessarily give up all that would separate us from Him. Hence the Saviour says, "Whosoever he be of you that forsaketh not all that he hath, he cannot be My disciple." Luke

14:33. Whatever shall draw away the heart from God must be given up. Mammon is the idol of many. The love of money, the desire for wealth, is the golden chain that binds them to Satan. Reputation and worldly honor are worshiped by another class. **The life of selfish ease and freedom from responsibility is the idol of others. But these slavish bands must be broken.** We cannot be half the Lord's and half the world's. We are not God's children unless we are such entirely.

There are those who profess to serve God, while they rely upon their own efforts to obey His law, to form a right character, and secure salvation. Their hearts are not moved by any deep sense of the love of Christ, but they seek to perform the duties of the Christian life as that which God requires of them in order to gain heaven. Such religion is worth nothing. **When Christ dwells in the heart, the soul will be so filled with His love, with the joy of communion with Him, that it will cleave to Him; and in the contemplation of Him, self will be forgotten.** Love to Christ will be the spring of action. **Those who feel the constraining love of God do not ask how little may be given to meet the requirements of God; they do not ask for the lowest standard, but aim at perfect conformity to the will of their Redeemer.** With earnest desire they yield all and manifest an interest proportionate to the value of the object which they seek. A profession of Christ without this deep love is mere talk, dry formality, and heavy drudgery.

Do you feel that it is too great a sacrifice to yield all to Christ? Ask yourself the question, "What has Christ given for me?" The Son of God gave all—life and love and suffering—for our redemption. **And can it be that we, the unworthy objects of so great love, will withhold our hearts from Him?** Every moment of our lives we have been partakers of the blessings of His grace, and for this very reason we cannot fully realize the depths of ignorance and misery from which we have been saved. **Can we look upon Him whom our sins have pierced, and yet be willing to do despite to all His love and sacrifice?** In view of the infinite humiliation of the Lord of glory, shall we murmur because we can enter into life only through conflict and self-abasement?

The inquiry of many a proud heart is, "Why need I go in penitence and humiliation before I can have the assurance of my acceptance with God?" I point you to Christ. He was sinless, and, more than this, He was the Prince of heaven; but in man's behalf He became sin for the race. "He was numbered with the transgressors; and He bare the sin of many, and made intercession for the transgressors." Isaiah 53:12.

But what do we give up, when we give all? A sin-polluted heart, for Jesus to purify, to cleanse by His own blood, and to save by His matchless love. And yet men think it hard to give up all! I am ashamed to hear it spoken of, ashamed to write it.

God does not require us to give up anything that it is for our best interest to retain. In all that He does, He has the well-being of His children in view. Would that all who have not chosen Christ might realize that He has something vastly better to offer them than they are seeking for themselves. **Man is doing the greatest injury and injustice to his own soul when he thinks and acts contrary to the will of God.** No real joy can be found in the path forbidden by Him who knows what is best and who plans for the good of His creatures. The path of transgression is the path of misery and destruction.

It is a mistake to entertain the thought that God is pleased to see His children suffer. All heaven is interested in the happiness of man. Our heavenly Father does not close the avenues of joy to any of His creatures. The divine requirements call upon us to shun those indulgences that would bring suffering and disappointment, that would close to us the door of happiness and heaven. **The world's Redeemer accepts men as they are, with all their wants, imperfections, and weaknesses**; and He will not only cleanse from sin and grant redemption through His blood, but will satisfy the heart-longing of all who consent to wear His yoke, to bear His burden. **It is His purpose to impart peace and rest to all who come to Him for the bread of life. He requires us to perform only those duties that will lead our steps to heights of bliss to which the disobedient can never attain.** The true, joyous life of the soul is to have Christ formed within, the hope of glory.

Many are inquiring, "*How* am I to make the surrender of myself to God?" You desire to give yourself to Him, but you are weak in moral power, in slavery to doubt, and controlled by the habits of your life of sin. Your promises and resolutions are like ropes of sand. You cannot control your thoughts, your impulses, your affections. The knowledge of your broken promises and forfeited pledges weakens your confidence in your own sincerity, and causes you to feel that God cannot accept you; but you need not despair. **What you need to understand is the true force of the will. This is the governing power in the nature of man, the power of decision, or of choice. Everything depends on the right action of the will.** The power of choice God has given to men; it is theirs to exercise. You cannot change your heart, you cannot of yourself give to God its affections; but **you can *choose* to serve Him. You can give Him your will; He will then work in you to will and to do according to His good pleasure.** Thus your whole nature will be brought under the control of the Spirit of Christ; your affections will be centered upon Him, your thoughts will be in harmony with Him.

Desires for goodness and holiness are right as far as they go; but if you stop here, they will avail nothing. Many will be lost while hoping and desiring to be Christians. They do not come to the point of yielding the will to God. They do not now choose to be Christians.

Through the right exercise of the will, an entire change may be made in your life. By yielding up your will to Christ, you ally yourself with the power that is above all principalities and powers. You will have strength from above to hold you steadfast, and thus through constant surrender to God you will be enabled to live the new life, even the life of faith.

Faith and Acceptance

As your conscience has been quickened by the Holy Spirit, you have seen something of the evil of sin, of its power, its guilt, its woe; and you look upon it with abhorrence. You feel that sin has separated you from God, that you are in bondage to the power of evil. The more you struggle to escape, the more you realize your helplessness. Your motives are impure; your heart is unclean. You see that your life has been filled with selfishness and sin. **You long to be forgiven, to be cleansed, to be set free. Harmony with God, likeness to Him—what can you do to obtain it?**

It is peace that you need—Heaven's forgiveness and peace and love in the soul. Money cannot buy it, intellect cannot procure it, wisdom cannot attain to it; you can never hope, by your own efforts, to secure it. But God offers it to you as a gift, "without money and without price" (Isaiah 55:1). **It is yours if you will but reach out your hand and grasp it.** The Lord says, "Though your sins be as scarlet, they shall be as white as snow; though they be red like crimson, they shall be as wool." Isaiah 1:18. "A new heart also will I give you, and a new spirit will I put within you." Ezekiel 36:26.

You have confessed your sins, and in heart put them away. You have resolved to give yourself to God. Now go to Him, and ask that He will wash away your sins and give you a new heart. Then believe that He does this *because He has promised.* This is the lesson which Jesus taught while He was on earth, that **the gift which God promises us we must believe we do receive, and it is ours.** Jesus healed the people of their diseases when they had faith in His power; He helped them in the things which they could see, thus inspiring them with confidence in Him concerning things which they could not see—leading them to believe in His power to forgive sins. This He plainly stated in the healing of the man sick with palsy: *"That ye may know that the Son of man hath power on earth to forgive sins.* Then saith He to the sick of the palsy, Arise, take up thy bed, and go unto thine house." Matthew 9:6. So also John the evangelist says, speaking of the miracles of Christ, **"These are written, that ye might believe that Jesus is the Christ, the Son of God; and that believing ye might have life through His name."** John 20:31.

From the simple Bible account of how Jesus healed the sick, we may learn something about how to believe in Him for the forgiveness of sins. Let us turn to the story of the paralytic at Bethesda. The poor sufferer was helpless; he had not used his limbs for thirty-eight years. Yet Jesus bade him, "Rise, take up thy bed, and walk." The sick man might have said, "Lord, if Thou wilt make me whole, I will obey Thy word." But, no, he believed Christ's word, believed that he was made whole, and he made the effort at once; he *willed* to walk, and he did walk. He acted on the word of Christ, and God gave the power. He was made whole.

In like manner you are a sinner. You cannot atone for your past sins; you cannot change your heart and make yourself holy. But God promises to do all this for you through Christ. You *believe* that promise. You confess your sins and give yourself to God. **You *will* to serve Him. Just as surely as you do this, God will fulfill His word to you. If you believe the promise,—believe that you are forgiven and cleansed,—God supplies the fact; you are made whole**, just as Christ gave the paralytic power to walk when the man believed that he was healed. It is so if you believe it.

Do not wait to *feel* that you are made whole, but say, "I believe it; it is so, not because I feel it, but because God has promised."

Jesus says, "What things soever ye desire, when ye pray, believe that ye receive them, and ye shall have them." Mark 11:24. **There is a condition to this promise— that we pray according to the will of God. But it is the will of God to cleanse us from sin, to make us His children, and to enable us to live a holy life.** So we may ask for these blessings, and believe that we receive them, and thank God that we have received them. **It is our privilege to go to Jesus and be cleansed, and to stand before the law without shame or remorse.** "There is therefore now no condemnation to them which are in Christ Jesus, who walk not after the flesh, but after the Spirit." Romans 8:1.

Henceforth you are not your own; you are bought with a price. "Ye were not redeemed with corruptible things, as silver and gold . . but with the precious blood of Christ, as of a lamb without blemish and without spot." 1 Peter 1:18-19. **Through this simple act of believing God, the Holy Spirit has begotten a new life in your heart.** You are as a child born into the family of God, and He loves you as He loves His Son.

Now that you have given yourself to Jesus, do not draw back, do not take yourself away from Him, but day by day say, "I am Christ's; I have given myself to Him"; and ask Him to give you His Spirit and keep you by His grace. **As it is by giving yourself to God, and believing Him, that you become His child, so you are to live in Him.** The apostle says, "As ye have therefore received Christ Jesus the Lord, so walk ye in Him." Colossians 2:6.

Some seem to feel that they must be on probation, and must prove to the Lord that they are reformed, before they can claim His blessing. But they may claim the blessing of God even now. They must have His grace, the Spirit of Christ, to help their infirmities, or they cannot resist evil. Jesus loves to have us come to Him just as we are, sinful, helpless, dependent. **We may come with all our weakness, our folly, our sinfulness, and fall at His feet in penitence. It is His glory to encircle us in the arms of His love and to bind up our wounds, to cleanse us from all impurity.**

Here is where thousands fail; they do not believe that Jesus pardons them personally, individually. They do not take God at His word. It is the privilege of all who comply with the conditions, to know for themselves that pardon is freely extended for every sin. Put away the suspicion that God's promises are not meant for you. They are for every repentant transgressor. Strength and grace have been provided through Christ to be brought by ministering angels to every believing soul. **None are so sinful that they cannot find strength, purity, and righteousness in Jesus, who died for them.** He is wait-

ing to strip them of their garments, stained and polluted with sin, and to put upon them the white robes of
righteousness; He bids them live and not die.

**God does not deal with us as finite men deal with
one another. His thoughts are thoughts of mercy, love,
and tenderest compassion.** He says, "Let the wicked
forsake his way, and the unrighteous man his thoughts:
and let him return unto the Lord, and He will have mercy
upon him; and to our God, for He will abundantly pardon" (Isaiah 55:7). "I have blotted out, as a thick cloud,
thy transgressions, and, as a cloud, thy sins." Isaiah
44:22.

"I have no pleasure in the death of him that dieth,
saith the Lord God: wherefore turn yourselves, and live
ye." Ezekiel 18:32. **Satan is ready to steal away the
blessed assurances of God. He desires to take every
glimmer of hope and every ray of light from the soul;
but you must not permit him to do this. Do not give
ear to the tempter, but say, "Jesus has died that I might
live. He loves me**, and wills not that I should perish. I
have a compassionate heavenly Father; and although I
have abused His love, though the blessings He has given
me have been squandered, **I will arise, and go to my
Father, and say, 'I have sinned against heaven, and
before Thee**, and am no more worthy to be called Thy
son: make me as one of Thy hired servants.' " The parable tells you how the wanderer will be received: *"When
he was yet a great way off,* his father saw him, and
had compassion, and ran, and fell on his neck, and kissed
him." Luke 15:18-20.

But even this parable, tender and touching as it is,
comes short of expressing the infinite compassion of the
heavenly Father. The Lord declares by His prophet, "I
have loved thee with an everlasting love: *therefore with
loving-kindness have I drawn thee."* Jeremiah 31:3.

While the sinner is yet far from the Father's house, wasting his substance in a strange country, the Father's heart is yearning over him; and every longing awakened in the soul to return to God is but the tender pleading of His Spirit, wooing, entreating, drawing the wanderer to his Father's heart of love.

With the rich promises of the Bible before you, can you give place to doubt? Can you believe that when the poor sinner longs to return, longs to forsake his sins, the Lord sternly withholds him from coming to His feet in repentance? Away with such thoughts! Nothing can hurt your own soul more than to entertain such a conception of our heavenly Father. He hates sin, but He loves the sinner, and He gave Himself in the person of Christ, that all who would might be saved and have eternal blessedness in the kingdom of glory. What stronger or more tender language could have been employed than He has chosen in which to express His love toward us? He declares, "Can a woman forget her sucking child, that she should not have compassion on the son of her womb? yea, they may forget, yet will I not forget thee." Isaiah 49:15.

Look up, you that are doubting and trembling; for Jesus lives to make intercession for us. Thank God for the gift of His dear Son and pray that He may not have died for you in vain. **The Spirit invites you today. Come with your whole heart to Jesus, and you may claim His blessing.**

As you read the promises, remember they are the expression of unutterable love and pity. The great heart of Infinite Love is drawn toward the sinner with boundless compassion. "We have redemption through His blood, the forgiveness of sins." Ephesians 1:7. Yes, only believe that God is your helper. He wants to restore His moral image in man. **As you draw near to Him with confes-**

sion and repentance, He will draw near to you with mercy and forgiveness.

The Test of Discipleship

"If any man be in Christ, he is a new creature: old things are passed away; behold, all things are become new." 2 Corinthians 5:17.

A person may not be able to tell the exact time or place, or trace all the chain of circumstances in the process of conversion; but this does not prove him to be unconverted. Christ said to Nicodemus, "The wind bloweth where it listeth, and thou hearest the sound thereof, but canst not tell whence it cometh, and whither it goeth: so is everyone that is born of the Spirit." John 3:8. Like the wind, which is invisible, yet the effects of which are plainly seen and felt, is the Spirit of God in its work upon the human heart. **That regenerating power, which no human eye can see, begets a new life in the soul; it creates a new being in the image of God.** While the work of the Spirit is silent and imperceptible, its effects are manifest. If the heart has been renewed by the Spirit of God, the life will bear witness to the fact. **While we cannot do anything to change our hearts or to bring ourselves into harmony with God; while we must not trust at all to ourselves or our good works, our lives will reveal whether the grace of God is dwelling within us.** A change will be seen in the character, the habits, the pursuits. The contrast will be clear and decided between what they have been and what they are. **The character is revealed, not by occasional good deeds and occasional misdeeds, but by the tendency of the habitual words and acts.**

It is true that there may be an outward correctness of deportment without the renewing power of Christ. The love of influence and the desire for the esteem of others may produce a well-ordered life. Self-respect may lead us to avoid the appearance of evil. A selfish heart may perform generous actions. **By what means, then, shall we determine whose side we are on?**

Who has the heart? With whom are our thoughts? Of whom do we love to converse? Who has our warmest affections and our best energies? If we are Christ's, our thoughts are with Him, and our sweetest thoughts are of Him. All we have and are is consecrated to Him. We long to bear His image, breathe His spirit, do His will, and please Him in all things.

Those who become new creatures in Christ Jesus will bring forth the fruits of the Spirit, "love, joy, peace, long-suffering, gentleness, goodness, faith, meekness, temperance." Galatians 5:22-23. **They will no longer fashion themselves according to the former lusts, but by the faith of the Son of God they will follow in His steps**, reflect His character, and purify themselves even as He is pure. **The things they once hated they now love, and the things they once loved they hate. The proud and self-assertive become meek and lowly in heart.** The vain and supercilious become serious and unobtrusive. The drunken becomes sober, and the profligate pure. **The vain customs and fashions of the world are laid aside.** Christians will seek not the "outward adorning," but "the hidden man of the heart, in that which is not corruptible, even the ornament of a meek and quiet spirit" (1 Peter 3:3-4).

There is no evidence of genuine repentance unless it works reformation. If he restore the pledge, give again that he had robbed, confess his sins, and love God and his fellow men, the sinner may be sure that he has passed from death unto life.

When, as erring, sinful beings, we come to Christ and become partakers of His pardoning grace, love springs up in the heart. Every burden is light, for the yoke that Christ imposes is easy. **Duty becomes a delight, and sacrifice a pleasure.** The path that before seemed shrouded in darkness, becomes bright with beams from the Sun of Righteousness.

The loveliness of the character of Christ will be seen in His followers. It was His delight to do the will of God. Love to God, zeal for His glory, was the controlling power in our Saviour's life. Love beautified and ennobled all His actions. **Love is of God. The unconsecrated heart cannot originate or produce it. It is found only in the heart where Jesus reigns.** "We love, because He first loved us." 1 John 4:19, R.V. In the heart renewed by divine grace, love is the principle of action. It modifies the character, governs the impulses, controls the passions, subdues enmity, and ennobles the affections. This love, cherished in the soul, sweetens the life and sheds a refining influence on all around.

There are two errors against which the children of God—particularly those who have just come to trust in His grace—especially need to guard. The first, already dwelt upon, is that of looking to their own works, trusting to anything they can do, to bring themselves into harmony with God. **He who is trying to become holy by his own works in keeping the law, is attempting an impossibility.** All that man can do without Christ is polluted with selfishness and sin. **It is the grace of Christ alone, through faith, that can make us holy.**

The opposite and no less dangerous error is that belief in Christ releases men from keeping the law of God; that since by faith alone we become partakers of the grace of Christ, our works have nothing to do with our redemption.

But notice here that **obedience is not a mere outward compliance, but the service of love.** The law of God is an expression of His very nature; it is an embodiment of the great principle of love, and hence is the foundation of His government in heaven and earth. **If our hearts are renewed in the likeness of God, if the divine love is implanted in the soul, will not the law of God be carried out in the life?** When the principle of love is implanted in the heart, when man is renewed after the image of Him that created him, the new-covenant promise is fulfilled, **"I will put My laws into their hearts, and in their minds will I write them."** Hebrews 10:16. And if the law is written in the heart, will it not shape the life? **Obedience—the service and allegiance of love—is the true sign of discipleship.** Thus the Scripture says, "This is the love of God, that we keep His commandments." 1 John 5:3 "He that saith, I know Him, and keepeth not His commandments, is a liar, and the truth is not in him." 1 John 2:4. **Instead of releasing man from obedience, it is faith, and faith only, that makes us partakers of the grace of Christ, which enables us to render obedience.**

We do not earn salvation by our obedience; for salvation is the free gift of God, to be received by faith. But obedience is the fruit of faith. "Ye know that He was manifested to take away our sins; and in Him is no sin. Whosoever abideth in Him sinneth not: whosoever sinneth hath not seen Him, neither known Him." 1 John 3:5-6. **Here is the true test. If we abide in Christ, if the love of God dwells in us, our feelings, our thoughts, our purposes, our actions, will be in harmony with the will of God as expressed in the precepts of His holy law.** "Little children, let no man deceive you: he that doeth righteousness is righteous, even as He is righteous."

1 John 3:7. **Righteousness is defined by the standard of God's holy law, as expressed in the ten precepts given on Sinai.**

That so-called faith in Christ which professes to release men from the obligation of obedience to God, is not faith, but presumption. "By grace are ye saved through faith." Ephesians 2:8. But "faith, if it hath not works, is dead." James 2:17. Jesus said of Himself before He came to earth, **"I delight to do Thy will, O My God: yea, Thy law is within My heart."** Psalm 40:8. And just before He ascended again to heaven He declared, "I have kept My Father's commandments, and abide in His love." John 15:10. The Scripture says, **"Hereby we do know that we know Him, if we keep His commandments** . . He that saith he abideth in Him ought himself also so to walk even as He walked." 1 John 2:3-6. "Because Christ also suffered for us, leaving us an example, that ye should follow His steps." 1 Peter 2:21.

The condition of eternal life is now just what it always has been,—just what it was in Paradise before the fall of our first parents,—perfect obedience to the law of God, perfect righteousness. If eternal life were granted on any condition short of this, then the happiness of the whole universe would be imperiled. The way would be open for sin, with all its train of woe and misery, to be immortalized.

It was possible for Adam, before the fall, to form a righteous character by obedience to God's law. But he failed to do this, and because of his sin our natures are fallen and we cannot make ourselves righteous. Since we are sinful, unholy, we cannot perfectly obey the holy law. **We have no righteousness of our own with which to meet the claims of the law of God.** But Christ has made a way of escape for us. He lived on earth amid trials and temptations such as we have to meet. He lived a sinless life. He died for us, and now He offers to take our sins and give us His righteousness. **If you give yourself to Him, and accept Him as your Saviour, then, sinful as your life may have been, for His sake you are accounted righteous. Christ's character stands in place of your character, and you are accepted before God just as if you had not sinned.**

More than this, Christ changes the heart. He abides in your heart by faith. **You are to maintain this connection with Christ by faith and the continual surrender of your will to Him; and so long as you do this, He will work in you to will and to do according to His good pleasure.** So you may say, "The life which I now live in the flesh I live by the faith of the Son of God, who loved me, and gave Himself for me." Galatians 2:20. So Jesus said to His disciples, "It is not ye that speak, but the Spirit of your Father which speaketh in you." Matthew 10:20. **Then with Christ working in you, you will manifest the same spirit and do the same good works—** works of righteousness, obedience.

So we have nothing in ourselves of which to boast. We have no ground for self-exaltation. Our only ground of hope is in the righteousness of Christ imputed to us, and in that wrought by His Spirit working in and through us.

When we speak of faith, there is a distinction that should be borne in mind. There is a kind of belief that is wholly distinct from faith. The existence and power of God, the truth of His Word, are facts that even Satan and his hosts cannot at heart deny. The Bible says that "the devils also believe, and tremble," but this is not faith (James 2:19). **Where there is not only a belief in God's Word, but a submission of the will to Him; where the heart is yielded to Him, the affections fixed upon Him, there is faith—faith that works by**

love and purifies the soul. Through this faith the heart is renewed in the image of God. And the heart that in its unrenewed state is not subject to the law of God, neither indeed can be, now delights in its holy precepts, exclaiming with the psalmist, "O how love I Thy law! It is my meditation all the day" (Psalm 119:97). And the righteousness of the law is fulfilled in us, "who walk not after the flesh, but after the Spirit." Romans 8:1.

There are those who have known the pardoning love of Christ and who really desire to be children of God, yet **they realize that their character is imperfect, their life faulty, and they are ready to doubt whether their hearts have been renewed by the Holy Spirit. To such I would say, Do not draw back in despair.** We shall often have to bow down and weep at the feet of Jesus because of our shortcomings and mistakes, but we are not to be discouraged. **Even if we are overcome by the enemy, we are not cast off, not forsaken and rejected of God.** No; Christ is at the right hand of God, who also maketh intercession for us. Said the beloved John, "These things write I unto you, that ye sin not. And if any man sin, we have an advocate with the Father, Jesus Christ the righteous." 1 John 2:1. And do not forget the words of Christ, "The Father Himself loveth you." John 16:27. **He desires to restore you to Himself, to see His own purity and holiness reflected in you. And if you will but yield yourself to Him, He that hath begun a good work in you will carry it forward to the day of Jesus Christ.** Pray more fervently; believe more fully. As we come to distrust our own power, let us trust the power of our Redeemer, and we shall praise Him who is the health of our countenance.

The closer you come to Jesus, the more faulty you will appear in your own eyes; for your vision will be clearer, and your imperfections will be seen in broad and distinct contrast to His perfect nature. **This is evidence that Satan's delusions have lost their power**; that the vivifying influence of the Spirit of God is arousing you.

No deep-seated love for Jesus can dwell in the heart that does not realize its own sinfulness. The soul that is transformed by the grace of Christ will admire His divine character; but if we do not see our own moral deformity, it is unmistakable evidence that we have not had a view of the beauty and excellence of Christ.

The less we see to esteem in ourselves, the more we shall see to esteem in the infinite purity and loveliness of our Saviour. A view of our sinfulness drives us to Him who can pardon; and when the soul, realizing its helplessness, reaches out after Christ, He will reveal Himself in power. **The more our sense of need drives us to Him and to the Word of God, the more exalted views we shall have of His character, and the more fully we shall reflect His image.**

Growing Up into Christ

The change of heart by which we become children of God is, in the Bible, spoken of as birth. Again, **it is compared to the germination of the good seed sown by the husbandman.** In like manner those who are just converted to Christ are, "as newborn babes" (1 Peter 2:2), to "grow up" (Ephesians 4:15) to the stature of men and women in Christ Jesus. Or like the good seed sown in the field, they are to grow up and bring forth fruit. Isaiah says that they shall "be called trees of righteousness, the planting of the Lord, that He might be glorified." Isaiah 61:3. So from natural life, illustra-

tions are drawn, to help us better to understand the
mysterious truths of spiritual life.

**Not all the wisdom and skill of man can produce
life in the smallest object in nature. It is only through
the life which God Himself has imparted, that either
plant or animal can live. So it is only through the life
from God that spiritual life is begotten in the hearts
of men.** Unless a man is "born from above," he cannot
become a partaker of the life which Christ came to give
(John 3:3, margin).

**As with life, so it is with growth. It is God who
brings the bud to bloom and the flower to fruit. It is
by His power that the seed develops**, "first the blade,
then the ear, after that the full corn in the ear" (Mark
4:28). And the prophet, Hosea, says of Israel, that "he
shall grow as the lily . . They shall revive as the corn,
and grow as the vine." Hosea 14:5, 7. And Jesus bids us
"consider the lilies how they grow." Luke 12:27. **The
plants and flowers grow not by their own care or anxiety or effort, but by receiving that which God has fur-
nished to minister to their life.** The child cannot, by
any anxiety or power of its own, add to its stature. **No
more can you, by anxiety or effort of yourself, secure
spiritual growth.** The plant, the child, grows by receiving from its surroundings that which ministers to its
life—air, sunshine, and food. What these gifts of nature
are to animal and plant, such is Christ to those who
trust in Him. He is their "everlasting light" (Isaiah 60:19),
"a sun and shield" (Psalm 84:11). He shall be as "the
dew unto Israel" (Hosea 14:5). "He shall come down like
rain upon the mown grass." Psalm 72:6. He is the living
water, "the Bread of God . . which cometh down from
heaven, and giveth life unto the world" (John 6:33).

**In the matchless gift of His Son, God has encircled
the whole world with an atmosphere of grace as real**

as the air which circulates around the globe. All who choose to breathe this life-giving atmosphere will live and grow up to the stature of men and women in Christ Jesus.

As the flower turns to the sun, that the bright beams may aid in perfecting its beauty and symmetry, so should we turn to the Sun of Righteousness, that heaven's light may shine upon us, that our character may be developed into the likeness of Christ.

Jesus teaches the same thing when He says, "Abide in Me, and I in you. **As the branch cannot bear fruit of itself, except it abide in the vine; no more can ye, except ye abide in Me . . Without Me ye can do nothing.**" John 15:4-5. You are just as dependent upon Christ, in order to live a holy life, as is the branch upon the parent stock for growth and fruitfulness. **Apart from Him you have no life. You have no power to resist temptation or to grow in grace and holiness. Abiding in Him, you may flourish.** Drawing your life from Him, you will not wither nor be fruitless. You will be like a tree planted by the rivers of water.

Many have an idea that they must do some part of the work alone. They have trusted in Christ for the forgiveness of sin, but now they seek by their own efforts to live aright. **But every such effort must fail.** Jesus says, "Without Me ye can do nothing." Our growth in grace, our joy, our usefulness,—all depend upon our union with Christ. **It is by communion with Him, daily, hourly,— by abiding in Him,—that we are to grow in grace. He is not only the Author, but the Finisher of our faith.** It is Christ first and last and always. He is to be with us, not only at the beginning and the end of our course, but at every step of the way. David says, "I have set the Lord always before me: because He is at my right hand, I shall not be moved." Psalm 16:8.

Do you ask, "How am I to abide in Christ?" In the

same way as you received Him at first. "As ye have therefore received Christ Jesus the Lord, so walk ye in Him." Colossians 2:6. "The just shall live by faith." Hebrews 10:38. **You gave yourself to God, to be His wholly, to serve and obey Him, and you took Christ as your Saviour.** You could not yourself atone for your sins or change your heart; but having given yourself to God, you believe that He, for Christ's sake, did all this for you. **By faith you became Christ's, and by *faith* you are to grow up in Him—by giving and taking. You are to give all,—your heart, your will, your service,—*give* yourself to Him to obey all His requirements; and you must *take* all,—Christ, the fullness of all blessing, to abide in your heart, to be your strength, your righteousness, your everlasting helper,—to give you power to obey.**

Consecrate yourself to God in the morning; make this your very first work. Let your prayer be, "Take me, O Lord, as wholly Thine. I lay all my plans at Thy feet. Use me today in Thy service. Abide with me, and let all my work be wrought in Thee." This is a daily matter. **Each morning consecrate yourself to God for that day. Surrender all your plans to Him, to be carried out or given up as His providence shall indicate.** Thus day by day you may be giving your life into the hands of God, and thus your life will be molded more and more after the life of Christ.

A life in Christ is a life of restfulness. There may be no ecstasy of feeling, but there should be an abiding, peaceful trust. Your hope is not in yourself; it is in Christ. Your weakness is united to His strength, your ignorance to His wisdom, your frailty to His enduring might. So you are not to look to yourself, not to let the mind dwell upon self, but look to Christ. **Let the mind dwell upon His love, upon the beauty, the perfection, of His character.** Christ in His self-denial, Christ in His humiliation, Christ in His purity and holiness, Christ in His matchless love—this is the subject for the soul's contemplation. It is by loving Him, copying Him, depending wholly upon Him, that you are to be transformed into His likeness.

Jesus says, "Abide in Me." These words convey the idea of rest, stability, confidence. Again He invites, **"Come unto Me . . and I will give you rest."** Matthew 11:28. The words of the psalmist express the same thought: "Rest in the Lord, and wait patiently for Him." Psalm 37:7. And Isaiah gives the assurance, "In quietness and in confidence shall be your strength." Isaiah 30:15. **This rest is not found in inactivity**; for in the Saviour's invitation the promise of rest is united with the call to labor: "Take My yoke upon you . . and ye shall find rest." Matthew 11:29. **The heart that rests most fully upon Christ will be most earnest and active in labor for Him.**

When the mind dwells upon self, it is turned away from Christ, the source of strength and life. Hence it is Satan's constant effort to keep the attention diverted from the Saviour and thus prevent the union and communion of the soul with Christ. **The pleasures of the world, life's cares and perplexities and sorrows, the faults of others, or your own faults and imperfections—to any or all of these he will seek to divert the mind.** Do not be misled by his devices. Many who are really conscientious, and who desire to live for God, he too often leads to dwell upon their own faults and weaknesses, and thus by separating them from Christ he hopes to gain the victory. **We should not make self the center and indulge anxiety and fear as to whether we shall be saved. All this turns the soul away from the Source of our strength.** Commit the keeping of your soul to God, and trust in Him. **Talk and think of Jesus.**

Let self be lost in Him. Put away all doubt; dismiss your fears. Say with the apostle Paul, "I live; yet not I, but Christ liveth in me: and the life which I now live in the flesh I live by the faith of the Son of God, who loved me, and gave Himself for me." Galatians 2:20. **Rest in God. He is able to keep that which you have committed to Him.** If you will leave yourself in His hands, He will bring you off more than conqueror through Him that has loved you.

When Christ took human nature upon Him, He bound humanity to Himself by a tie of love that can never be broken by any power save the choice of man himself. Satan will constantly present allurements to induce us to break this tie—to choose to separate ourselves from Christ. **Here is where we need to watch, to strive, to pray, that nothing may entice us to** *choose* **another master; for we are always free to do this. But let us keep our eyes fixed upon Christ, and He will preserve us.** Looking unto Jesus, we are safe. Nothing can pluck us out of His hand. In constantly beholding Him, we "are changed into the same image from glory to glory, even as by the Spirit of the Lord." 2 Corinthians 3:18.

It was thus that the early disciples gained their likeness to the dear Saviour. **When those disciples heard the words of Jesus, they felt their need of Him. They sought, they found, they followed Him.** They were with Him in the house, at the table, in the closet, in the field. They were with Him as pupils with a teacher, daily receiving from His lips lessons of holy truth. They looked to Him, as servants to their master, to learn their duty. Those disciples were men "subject to like passions as we are" (James 5:17). **They had the same battle with sin to fight. They needed the same grace, in order to live a holy life.**

Even John, the beloved disciple, the one who most

fully reflected the likeness of the Saviour, did not naturally possess that loveliness of character. He was not only self-assertive and ambitious for honor, but impetuous, and resentful under injuries. But as the character of the Divine One was manifested to him, he saw his own deficiency and was humbled by the knowledge. The strength and patience, the power and tenderness, the majesty and meekness, that he beheld in the daily life of the Son of God, filled his soul with admiration and love. **Day by day his heart was drawn out toward Christ, until he lost sight of self in love for his Master. His resentful, ambitious temper was yielded to the molding power of Christ.** The regenerating influence of the Holy Spirit renewed his heart. **The power of the love of Christ wrought a transformation of character. This is the sure result of union with Jesus. When Christ abides in the heart, the whole nature is transformed.** Christ's Spirit, His love, softens the heart, subdues the soul, and raises the thoughts and desires toward God and heaven.

When Christ ascended to heaven, the sense of His presence was still with His followers. It was a personal presence, full of love and light. Jesus, the Saviour, who had walked and talked and prayed with them, who had spoken hope and comfort to their hearts, had, while the message of peace was still upon His lips, been taken up from them into heaven, and the tones of His voice had come back to them, as the cloud of angels received Him— "Lo, I am with you alway, even unto the end of the world" (Matthew 28:20). **He had ascended to heaven in the form of humanity. They knew that He was before the throne of God, their Friend and Saviour still; that His sympathies were unchanged; that He was still identified with suffering humanity.** He was presenting before God the merits of His own precious blood, showing His wounded hands and feet, in remembrance of the price

He had paid for His redeemed. **They knew that He had ascended to heaven to prepare places for them, and that He would come again and take them to Himself.**

As they met together after the ascension they were eager to present their requests to the Father in the name of Jesus. In solemn awe they bowed in prayer, repeating the assurance, "Whatsoever ye shall ask the Father in My name, He will give it you. Hitherto have ye asked nothing in My name: ask, and ye shall receive, that your joy may be full." John 16:23-24. **They extended the hand of faith higher and higher with the mighty argument, "It is Christ that died, yea rather, that is risen again, who is even at the right hand of God, who also maketh intercession for us"** (Romans 8:34). And Pentecost brought them the presence of the Comforter, of whom Christ had said, He "shall be in you." (John 14:17). And He had further said, "It is expedient for you that I go away: for if I go not away, the Comforter will not come unto you; but if I depart, I will send Him unto you." John 16:7. **Henceforth through the Spirit, Christ was to abide continually in the hearts of His children. Their union with Him was closer than when He was personally with them.** The light, and love, and power of the indwelling Christ shone out through them, so that men, beholding, "marveled; and they took knowledge of them, that they had been with Jesus" (Acts 4:13).

All that Christ was to the disciples, He desires to be to His children today; for in that last prayer, with the little band of disciples gathered about Him, He said, "Neither pray I for these alone, but for them also which shall believe on Me through their word." John 17:20.

Jesus prayed for us, and He asked that we might be one with Him, even as He is one with the Father. What a union is this! The Saviour has said of Himself, "The Son can do nothing of Himself" (John 5:19); "the

Father that dwelleth in Me, He doeth the works" (John 14:10). **Then if Christ is dwelling in our hearts, He will work in us "both to will and to do of His good pleasure."** Philippians 2:13. We shall work as He worked; we shall manifest the same spirit. And thus, loving Him and abiding in Him, we shall "grow up into Him in all things, which is the head, even Christ" (Ephesians 4:15).

The Work and the Life

God is the source of life and light and joy to the universe. Like rays of light from the sun, like the streams of water bursting from a living spring, blessings flow out from Him to all His creatures. **And wherever the life of God is in the hearts of men, it will flow out to others in love and blessing.**

Our Saviour's joy was in the uplifting and redemption of fallen men. For this He counted not His life dear unto Himself, but endured the cross, despising the shame. So angels are ever engaged in working for the happiness of others. This is their joy. That which selfish hearts would regard as humiliating service, ministering to those who are wretched and in every way inferior in character and rank is the work of sinless angels. **The spirit of Christ's self-sacrificing love is the spirit that pervades heaven and is the very essence of its bliss. This is the spirit that Christ's followers will possess, the work that they will do.**

When the love of Christ is enshrined in the heart, like sweet fragrance it cannot be hidden. Its holy influence will be felt by all with whom we come in contact. The spirit of Christ in the heart is like a spring in the desert, flowing to refresh all and making those who are ready to perish eager to drink of the water of life.

Love to Jesus will be manifested in a desire to work as He worked for the blessing and uplifting of humanity. It will lead to love, tenderness, and sympathy toward all the creatures of our heavenly Father's care.

The Saviour's life on earth was not a life of ease and devotion to Himself, but He toiled with persistent, earnest, untiring effort for the salvation of lost mankind. From the manger to Calvary He followed the path of self-denial and sought not to be released from arduous tasks, painful travels, and exhausting care and labor. He said, "The Son of man came not to be ministered unto, but to minister, and to give His life a ransom for many." Matthew 20:28. This was the one great object of His life. Everything else was secondary and subservient. It was His meat and drink to do the will of God and to finish His work. Self and self-interest had no part in His labor.

So those who are the partakers of the grace of Christ will be ready to make any sacrifice, that others for whom He died may share the heavenly gift. They will do all they can to make the world better for their stay in it. **This spirit is the sure outgrowth of a soul truly converted. No sooner does one come to Christ than there is born in his heart a desire to make known to others what a precious friend he has found in Jesus;** the saving and sanctifying truth cannot be shut up in his heart. **If we are clothed with the righteousness of Christ and are filled with the joy of His indwelling Spirit, we shall not be able to hold our peace.** If we have tasted and seen that the Lord is good we shall have something to tell. Like Philip when he found the Saviour, we shall invite others into His presence. We shall seek to present to them the attractions of Christ and the unseen realities of the world to come. **There will be an intensity of desire to follow in the path that Jesus trod.** There will be an earnest longing that those around us may "behold the Lamb of God, which taketh away the sin of the world" (John 1:29).

And the effort to bless others will react in blessings upon ourselves. This was the purpose of God in giving us a part to act in the plan of redemption. He has granted men the privilege of becoming partakers of the divine nature and, in their turn, of diffusing blessings to their fellow men. **This is the highest honor, the greatest joy, that it is possible for God to bestow upon men. Those who thus become participants in labors of love are brought nearest to their Creator.**

God might have committed the message of the gospel and all the work of loving ministry to the heavenly angels. He might have employed other means for accomplishing His purpose. **But, in His infinite love, He chose to make us co-workers with Himself, with Christ and the angels, that we might share the blessing, the joy, the spiritual uplifting, which results from this unselfish ministry.**

We are brought into sympathy with Christ through the fellowship of His sufferings. Every act of self-sacrifice for the good of others strengthens the spirit of beneficence in the giver's heart, allying him more closely to the Redeemer of the world, who "was rich, yet for your sakes . . became poor, that ye through His poverty might be rich" (2 Corinthians 8:9). **And it is only as we thus fulfill the divine purpose in our creation that life can be a blessing to us.**

If you will go to work as Christ designs that His disciples shall, and win souls for Him, you will feel the need of a deeper experience and a greater knowledge in divine things, and will hunger and thirst after righteousness. You will plead with God, and your faith will be strengthened, and your soul will drink deeper drafts at the well of salvation. **Encountering opposition and trials will drive you to the Bible and prayer. You will grow in grace and the knowledge of Christ, and will develop a rich experience.**

The spirit of unselfish labor for others gives depth, stability, and Christlike loveliness to the character, and brings peace and happiness to its possessor. The aspirations are elevated. There is no room for sloth or selfishness. Those who thus exercise the Christian graces will grow and will become strong to work for God. They will have clear spiritual perceptions, a steady, growing faith, and an increased power in prayer. The Spirit of God, moving upon their spirit, calls forth the sacred harmonies of the soul in answer to the divine touch. **Those who thus devote themselves to unselfish effort for the good of others are most surely working out their own salvation.**

The only way to grow in grace is to be disinterestedly doing the very work which Christ has enjoined upon us—to engage, to the extent of our ability, in helping and blessing those who need the help we can give them. Strength comes by exercise; activity is the very condition of life. Those who endeavor to maintain Christian life by passively accepting the blessings that come through the means of grace, and doing nothing for Christ, are simply trying to live by eating without working. And in the spiritual as in the natural world, this always results in degeneration and decay. A man who would refuse to exercise his limbs would soon lose all power to use them. **Thus the Christian who will not exercise his God-given powers not only fails to grow up into Christ, but he loses the strength that he already had.**

The church of Christ is God's appointed agency

for the salvation of men. Its mission is to carry the gospel to the world.** And the obligation rests upon all Christians. Everyone, to the extent of his talent and opportunity, is to fulfill the Saviour's commission. The love of Christ, revealed to us, makes us debtors to all who know Him not. **God has given us light, not for ourselves alone, but to shed upon them.**

If the followers of Christ were awake to duty, there would be thousands where there is one today proclaiming the gospel in heathen lands. And all who could not personally engage in the work would yet sustain it with their means, their sympathy, and their prayers. And there would be far more earnest labor for souls in Christian countries.

We need not go to heathen lands, or even leave the narrow circle of the home, if it is there that our duty lies, in order to work for Christ. We can do this in the home circle, in the church, among those with whom we associate, and with whom we do business.

The greater part of our Saviour's life on earth was spent in patient toil in the carpenter's shop at Nazareth. Ministering angels attended the Lord of life as He walked side by side with peasants and laborers, unrecognized and unhonored. He was as faithfully fulfilling His mission while working at His humble trade as when He healed the sick or walked upon the storm-tossed waves of Galilee. **So in the humblest duties and lowliest positions of life, we may walk and work with Jesus.**

The apostle says, "Let every man, wherein he is called, therein abide with God." 1 Corinthians 7:24. **The businessman may conduct his business in a way that will glorify his Master because of his fidelity.** If he is a true follower of Christ, he will carry his religion into everything that is done and reveal to men the spirit of Christ. **The mechanic may be a diligent and faithful repre-**

sentative of Him who toiled in the lowly walks of life among the hills of Galilee. Everyone who names the name of Christ should so work that others, by seeing his good works, may be led to glorify their Creator and Redeemer.

Many have excused themselves from rendering their gifts to the service of Christ because others were possessed of superior endowments and advantages. The opinion has prevailed that only those who are especially talented are required to consecrate their abilities to the service of God. It has come to be understood by many that talents are given to only a certain favored class to the exclusion of others who of course are not called upon to share in the toils or the rewards. But it is not so represented in the parable. **When the master of the house called his servants, he gave to every man** *his* **work.**

With a loving spirit we may perform life's humblest duties "as to the Lord" (Colossians 3:23). **If the love of God is in the heart, it will be manifested in the life.** The sweet savor of Christ will surround us, and our influence will elevate and bless.

You are not to wait for great occasions or to expect extraordinary abilities before you go to work for God. You need not have a thought of what the world will think of you. If your daily life is a testimony to the purity and sincerity of your faith, and others are convinced that you desire to benefit them, your efforts will not be wholly lost.

The humblest and poorest of the disciples of Jesus can be a blessing to others. They may not realize that they are doing any special good, but by their unconscious influence they may start waves of blessing that will widen and deepen, and the blessed results they may never know until the day of final reward. They do not feel or know that they are doing anything great. **They are not required to weary themselves with anxiety about**

success. **They have only to go forward quietly, doing
faithfully the work that God's providence assigns**, and
their life will not be in vain. Their own souls will be
growing more and more into the likeness of Christ; they
are workers together with God in this life and are thus
fitting for the higher work and the unshadowed joy of
the life to come.

A Knowledge of God

**Many are the ways in which God is seeking to make
Himself known to us and bring us into communion
with Him. Nature speaks to our senses without ceas-
ing.** The open heart will be impressed with the love and
glory of God as revealed through the works of His hands.
The listening ear can hear and understand the commu-
nications of God through the things of nature. The green
fields, the lofty trees, the buds and flowers, the passing
cloud, the falling rain, the babbling brook, the glories of
the heavens, speak to our hearts, and invite us to become acquainted with Him who made them all.

**Our Saviour bound up His precious lessons with
the things of nature.** The trees, the birds, the flowers
of the valleys, the hills, the lakes, and the beautiful heavens, as well as the incidents and surroundings of daily
life, were all linked with the words of truth, that His
lessons might thus be often recalled to mind, even amid
the busy cares of man's life of toil.

**God would have His children appreciate His works
and delight in the simple, quiet beauty with which He
has adorned our earthly home.** He is a lover of the beautiful. **And above all that is outwardly attractive, He
loves beauty of character; He would have us cultivate**

purity and simplicity, the quiet graces of the flowers.

If we will but listen, God's created works will teach us precious lessons of obedience and trust. From the stars that in their trackless courses through space follow from age to age their appointed path, down to the minutest atom, the things of nature obey the Creator's will. And God cares for everything and sustains everything that He has created. **He who upholds the unnumbered worlds throughout immensity, at the same time cares for the wants of the little brown sparrow that sings its humble song without fear.** When men go forth to their daily toil, as when they engage in prayer; when they lie down at night, and when they rise in the morning; when the rich man feasts in his palace, or when the poor man gathers his children about the scanty board, each is tenderly watched by the heavenly Father. **No tears are shed that God does not notice. There is no smile that He does not mark.**

If we would but fully believe this, all undue anxieties would be dismissed. Our lives would not be so filled with disappointment as now; for everything, whether great or small, would be left in the hands of God, who is not perplexed by the multiplicity of cares, or overwhelmed by their weight. **We should then enjoy a rest of soul to which many have long been strangers.**

As your senses delight in the attractive loveliness of the earth, think of the world that is to come, that shall never know the blight of sin and death; where the face of nature will no more wear the shadow of the curse. Let your imagination picture the home of the saved, and remember that it will be more glorious than your brightest imagination can portray. In the varied gifts of God in nature we see but the faintest gleaming of His glory. It is written, "Eye hath not seen, nor ear heard, neither have entered into the heart of man, the things which God hath prepared for them that love Him." 1 Corinthians 2:9.

The poet and the naturalist have many things to say about nature, but **it is the Christian who enjoys the beauty of the earth with the highest appreciation**, because he recognizes his Father's handiwork and perceives His love in flower and shrub and tree. **No one can fully appreciate the significance of hill and vale, river and sea, who does not look upon them as an expression of God's love to man.**

God speaks to us through His providential workings and through the influence of His Spirit upon the heart. In our circumstances and surroundings, in the changes daily taking place around us, we may find precious lessons if our hearts are but open to discern them. The psalmist, tracing the work of God's providence, says, "The earth is full of the goodness of the Lord." Psalm 33:5. "Whoso is wise, and will observe these things, even they shall understand the loving-kindness of the Lord." Psalm 107:43.

God speaks to us in His Word. Here we have in clearer lines the revelation of His character, of His dealings with men, and the great work of redemption. Here is open before us the history of patriarchs and prophets and other holy men of old. They were men "subject to like passions as we are" (James 5:17). **We see how they struggled through discouragements like our own, how they fell under temptation as we have done, and yet took heart again and conquered through the grace of God**; and, beholding, we are encouraged in our striving after righteousness. As we read of the precious experiences granted them, of the light and love and blessing it was theirs to enjoy, and of the work they wrought through the grace given them, the spirit that inspired them kindles a flame of holy emulation in our hearts and a desire to be like them in character—like them to walk with God.

Jesus said of the Old Testament Scriptures,—and how much more is it true of the New,—"They are they which testify of Me" (John 5:39), the Redeemer, Him in whom our hopes of eternal life are centered. **Yes, the whole Bible tells of Christ.** From the first record of creation—for "without Him was not anything made that was made" (John 1:3)—to the closing promise, "Behold, I come quickly" (Revelation 22:12), we are reading of His works and listening to His voice. **If you would become acquainted with the Saviour, study the Holy Scriptures.**

Fill the whole heart with the words of God. They are the living water, quenching your burning thirst. They are the living bread from heaven. Jesus declares, "Except ye eat the flesh of the Son of man, and drink His blood, ye have no life in you." And He explains Himself by saying, "The words that I speak unto you, they are spirit, and they are life." John 6:53, 63. Our bodies are built up from what we eat and drink; and as in the natural economy, so in the spiritual economy: **It is what we meditate upon that will give tone and strength to our spiritual nature.**

The theme of redemption is one that the angels desire to look into; it will be the science and the song of the redeemed throughout the ceaseless ages of eternity. Is it not worthy of careful thought and study now? The infinite mercy and love of Jesus, the sacrifice made in our behalf, call for the most serious and solemn reflection. We should dwell upon the character of our dear Redeemer and Intercessor. We should meditate upon the mission of Him who came to save His people from their sins. **As we thus contemplate heavenly themes, our faith and love will grow stronger, and our prayers will**

be more and more acceptable to God, because they will be more and more mixed with faith and love. They will be intelligent and fervent. There will be more constant confidence in Jesus and a daily, living experience in His power to save to the uttermost all that come unto God by Him.

As we meditate upon the perfections of the Saviour, we shall desire to be wholly transformed and renewed in the image of His purity. There will be a hungering and thirsting of soul to become like Him whom we adore. The more our thoughts are upon Christ, the more we shall speak of Him to others and represent Him to the world.

The Bible was not written for the scholar alone; on the contrary, it was designed for the common people. **The great truths necessary for salvation are made as clear as noonday; and none will mistake and lose their way except those who follow their own judgment instead of the plainly revealed will of God.**

We should not take the testimony of any man as to what the Scriptures teach, but should study the words of God for ourselves. If we allow others to do our thinking, we shall have crippled energies and contracted abilities. The noble powers of the mind may be so dwarfed by lack of exercise on themes worthy of their concentration as to lose their ability to grasp the deep meaning of the Word of God. **The mind will enlarge if it is employed in tracing out the relation of the subjects of the Bible, comparing Scripture with Scripture** and spiritual things with spiritual.

There is nothing more calculated to strengthen the intellect than the study of the Scriptures. No other book is so potent to elevate the thoughts, to give vigor to the faculties, as the broad, ennobling truths of the Bible. If God's Word were studied as it should be, men would have a breadth of mind, a nobility of character, and a stability of purpose rarely seen in these times.

But there is but little benefit derived from a hasty reading of the Scriptures. One may read the whole Bible through and yet fail to see its beauty or comprehend its deep and hidden meaning. **One passage studied until its significance is clear to the mind and its relation to the plan of salvation is of more value than the perusal of many chapters with no definite purpose** in view and no positive instruction gained. Keep your Bible with you. **As you have opportunity, read it; fix the texts in your memory. Even while you are walking the streets you may read a passage and meditate upon it**, thus fixing it in the mind.

We cannot obtain wisdom without earnest attention and prayerful study. Some portions of Scripture are indeed too plain to be misunderstood, but there are others whose meaning does not lie on the surface to be seen at a glance. **Scripture must be compared with Scripture. There must be careful research and prayerful reflection. And such study will be richly repaid.** As the miner discovers veins of precious metal concealed beneath the surface of the earth, so will he who perseveringly searches the Word of God as for hid treasure find truths of the greatest value, which are concealed from the view of the careless seeker. **The words of inspiration, pondered in the heart, will be as streams flowing from the fountain of life.**

Never should the Bible be studied without prayer. Before opening its pages we should ask for the enlightenment of the Holy Spirit, and it will be given. When Nathanael came to Jesus, the Saviour exclaimed, "Behold an Israelite indeed, in whom is no guile!" Nathanael said, "Whence knowest Thou me?" Jesus answered, "Before that Philip called thee, when thou wast under the fig tree, I saw thee" (John 1:47-48). **And Jesus will see us also in the secret places of prayer if we will seek Him for light that we may know what is truth. Angels from the world of light will be with those who in humility of heart seek for divine guidance.**

The Holy Spirit exalts and glorifies the Saviour. It is His office to present Christ, the purity of His righteousness, and the great salvation that we have through Him. Jesus says, "He shall receive of Mine, and shall show it unto you." John 16:14. **The Spirit of truth is the only effectual teacher of divine truth. How must God esteem the human race, since He gave His Son to die for them and appoints His Spirit to be man's teacher and continual guide!**

The Privilege of Prayer

Through nature and revelation, through His providence, and by the influence of His Spirit, God speaks to us. But these are not enough; we need also to pour out our hearts to Him. In order to have spiritual life and energy, we must have actual intercourse with our heavenly Father. Our minds may be drawn out toward Him; we may meditate upon His works, His mercies, His blessings; but this is not, in the fullest sense, communing with Him. **In order to commune with God, we must have something to say to Him concerning our actual life.**

Prayer is the opening of the heart to God as to a friend. Not that it is necessary in order to make known to God what we are, but in order to enable us to receive Him. **Prayer does not bring God down to us, but brings us up to Him.**

When Jesus was upon the earth, He taught His disciples how to pray. **He directed them to present their daily needs before God, and to cast all their care upon Him. And the assurance He gave them, that their petitions should be heard, is assurance also to us.**

Jesus Himself, while He dwelt among men, was often in prayer. Our Saviour identified Himself with our needs and weakness, in that **He became a suppliant, a petitioner, seeking from His Father fresh supplies of strength, that He might come forth braced for duty and trial. He is our example in all things.** He is a brother in our infirmities, "in all points tempted like as we are"; but as the sinless one His nature recoiled from evil; He endured struggles and torture of soul in a world of sin. His humanity made prayer a necessity and a privilege. **He found comfort and joy in communion with His Father.** And if the Saviour of men, the Son of God, felt the need of prayer, how much more should feeble, sinful mortals feel the necessity of fervent, constant prayer.

Our heavenly Father waits to bestow upon us the fullness of His blessing. It is our privilege to drink largely at the fountain of boundless love. What a wonder it is that we pray so little! **God is ready and willing to hear the sincere prayer of the humblest of His children**, and yet there is much manifest reluctance on our part to make known our wants to God. What can the angels of heaven think of poor helpless human beings, who are subject to temptation, when God's heart of infinite love yearns toward them, ready to give them more than they can ask or think, and yet they pray so little and have so little faith? **The angels love to bow before God; they love to be near Him. They regard communion with God as their highest joy; and yet the children of earth, who need so much the help that God only can give, seem satisfied to walk without the light**

of His Spirit, the companionship of His presence.

The darkness of the evil one encloses those who neglect to pray. The whispered temptations of the enemy entice them to sin; and it is all because they do not make use of the privileges that God has given them in the divine appointment of prayer. **Why should the sons and daughters of God be reluctant to pray, when prayer is the key in the hand of faith to unlock heaven's storehouse, where are treasured the boundless resources of Omnipotence?** Without unceasing prayer and diligent watching we are in danger of growing careless and of deviating from the right path. The adversary seeks continually to obstruct the way to the mercy seat, that we may not by earnest supplication and faith obtain grace and power to resist temptation.

There are certain conditions upon which we may expect that God will hear and answer our prayers. One of the first of these is that we feel our need of help from Him. He has promised, "I will pour water upon him that is thirsty, and floods upon the dry ground." Isaiah 44:3. **Those who hunger and thirst after righteousness, who long after God, may be sure that they will be filled.** The heart must be open to the Spirit's influence, or God's blessing cannot be received.

Our great need is itself an argument and pleads most eloquently in our behalf. But the Lord is to be sought unto to do these things for us. He says, "Ask, and it shall be given you." Matthew 7:7. And "He that spared not His own Son, but delivered Him up for us all, how shall He not with Him also freely give us all things?" Romans 8:32.

If we regard iniquity in our hearts, if we cling to any known sin, the Lord will not hear us; but the prayer of the penitent, contrite soul is always accepted. When all known wrongs are righted, we may believe that

God will answer our petitions. Our own merit will never commend us to the favor of God; it is the worthiness of Jesus that will save us, His blood that will cleanse us; yet we have a work to do in complying with the conditions of acceptance.

Another element of prevailing prayer is faith. "He that cometh to God must believe that He is, and that He is a rewarder of them that diligently seek Him." Hebrews 11:6. Jesus said to His disciples, "What things soever ye desire, when ye pray, believe that ye receive them, and ye shall have them." Mark 11:24. Do we take Him at His word?

The assurance is broad and unlimited, and He is faithful who has promised. **When we do not receive the very things we asked for, at the time we ask, we are still to believe that the Lord hears and that He will answer our prayers.** We are so erring and short-sighted that we sometimes ask for things that would not be a blessing to us, and **our heavenly Father in love answers our prayers by giving us that which will be for our highest good—that which we ourselves would desire if with vision divinely enlightened we could see all things as they really are.** When our prayers seem not to be answered, **we are to cling to the promise; for the time of answering will surely come**, and we shall receive the blessing we need most. **But to claim that prayer will always be answered in the very way and for the particular thing that we desire, is presumption.** God is too wise to err, and too good to withhold any good thing from them that walk uprightly. Then do not fear to trust Him, even though you do not see the immediate answer to your prayers. Rely upon His sure promise, "Ask, and it shall be given you" (Matthew 7:7).

If we take counsel with our doubts and fears, or try to solve everything that we cannot see clearly, before we have faith, perplexities will only increase and

deepen. But if we come to God, feeling helpless and dependent, as we really are, and in humble, trusting faith make known our wants to Him whose knowledge is infinite, who sees everything in creation, and who governs everything by His will and word, He can and will attend to our cry, and will let light shine into our hearts. **Through sincere prayer we are brought into connection with the mind of the Infinite.** We may have no remarkable evidence at the time that the face of our Redeemer is bending over us in compassion and love, but this is even so. We may not feel His visible touch, but His hand is upon us in love and pitying tenderness.

When we come to ask mercy and blessing from God we should have a spirit of love and forgiveness in our own hearts. How can we pray, "Forgive us our debts, as we forgive our debtors" (Matthew 6:12), and yet indulge an unforgiving spirit? **If we expect our own prayers to be heard we must forgive others in the same manner and to the same extent as we hope to be forgiven.**

Perseverance in prayer has been made a condition of receiving. We must pray always if we would grow in faith and experience. We are to be "instant in prayer" (Romans 12:12), to "continue in prayer, and watch in the same with thanksgiving" (Colossians 4:2). Peter exhorts believers to be "sober, and watch unto prayer." 1 Peter 4:7. Paul directs, "In everything by prayer and supplication with thanksgiving let your requests be made known unto God." Philippians 4:6. "But ye, beloved," says Jude, "praying in the Holy Ghost, keep yourselves in the love of God." Jude 20-21. **Unceasing prayer is the unbroken union of the soul with God, so that life from God flows into our life; and from our life, purity and holiness flow back to God.**

There is necessity for diligence in prayer; let nothing hinder you. **Make every effort to keep open the com-**

munion between Jesus and your own soul. **Seek every opportunity to go where prayer is wont to be made. Those who are really seeking for communion with God will be seen in the prayer meeting**, faithful to do their duty and earnest and anxious to reap all the benefits they can gain. They will improve every opportunity of placing themselves where they can receive the rays of light from heaven.

We should pray in the family circle, and above all we must not neglect secret prayer, for this is the life of the soul. It is impossible for the soul to flourish while prayer is neglected. Family or public prayer alone is not sufficient. In solitude let the soul be laid open to the inspecting eye of God. Secret prayer is to be heard only by the prayer-hearing God. No curious ear is to receive the burden of such petitions. **In secret prayer the soul is free from surrounding influences, free from excitement. Calmly, yet fervently, will it reach out after God.** Sweet and abiding will be the influence emanating from Him who seeth in secret, whose ear is open to hear the prayer arising from the heart. **By calm, simple faith the soul holds communion with God and gathers to itself rays of divine light to strengthen and sustain it in the conflict with Satan.** God is our tower of strength.

Pray in your closet, and as you go about your daily labor let your heart be often uplifted to God. It was thus that Enoch walked with God. **These silent prayers rise like precious incense before the throne of grace. Satan cannot overcome him whose heart is thus stayed upon God.**

There is no time or place in which it is inappropriate to offer up a petition to God. There is nothing that can prevent us from lifting up our hearts in the spirit of earnest prayer. In the crowds of the street, in the midst of a business engagement, we may send up a petition to God and plead for divine guidance, as did Nehemiah when he made his request before King Artaxerxes. A closet of communion may be found wherever we are. **We should have the door of the heart open continually and our invitation going up that Jesus may come and abide as a heavenly guest in the soul.**

Although there may be a tainted, corrupted atmosphere around us, we need not breathe its miasma, but may live in the pure air of heaven. **We may close every door to impure imaginings and unholy thoughts by lifting the soul into the presence of God through sincere prayer.** Those whose hearts are open to receive the support and blessing of God will walk in a holier atmosphere than that of earth and will have constant communion with heaven.

We need to have more distinct views of Jesus and a fuller comprehension of the value of eternal realities. The beauty of holiness is to fill the hearts of God's children; and that this may be accomplished, we should seek for divine disclosures of heavenly things.

Let the soul be drawn out and upward, that God may grant us a breath of the heavenly atmosphere. We may keep so near to God that, in every unexpected trial, our thoughts will turn to Him as naturally as the flower turns to the sun.

Keep your wants, your joys, your sorrows, your cares, and your fears before God. You cannot burden Him; you cannot weary Him. He who numbers the hairs of your head is not indifferent to the wants of His children. "The Lord is very pitiful, and of tender mercy." James 5:11. His heart of love is touched by our sorrows and even by our utterances of them. **Take to Him everything that perplexes the mind. Nothing is too great for Him to bear, for He holds up worlds**, He rules over all the affairs of the universe. Nothing that in any way concerns our peace is too small for Him to notice. There is no chapter in our experience too dark for Him to read; there is no perplexity too difficult for Him to unravel. No calamity can befall the least of His children, no anxiety harass the soul, no joy cheer, no sincere prayer escape the lips, of which our heavenly Father is unobservant, or in which He takes no immediate interest. "He healeth the broken in heart, and bindeth up their wounds." Psalm 147:3. **The relation between God and each soul is as distinct and full as though there were not another soul upon the earth to share His watchcare, not another soul for whom He gave His beloved Son.**

Jesus said, "Ye shall ask in My name: and I say not unto you, that I will pray the Father for you: for the Father Himself loveth you." John 16:26-27. "I have chosen you . . that whatsoever ye shall ask of the Father in My name, He may give it you." John 15:16. **But to pray in the name of Jesus is something more than a mere mention of that name at the beginning and the ending of a prayer. It is to pray in the mind and spirit of Jesus, while we believe His promises, rely upon His grace, and work His works.**

God does not mean that any of us should become hermits or monks and retire from the world in order to devote ourselves to acts of worship. **The life must be like Christ's life—between the mountain and the multitude. He who does nothing but pray will soon cease to pray, or his prayers will become a formal routine.** When men take themselves out of social life, away from the sphere of Christian duty and cross bearing, when they cease to work earnestly for the Master who worked earnestly for them, they lose the subject matter of prayer and have no incentive to devotion. Their prayers become personal and selfish. They cannot pray in regard to the wants of humanity or the upbuilding of Christ's kingdom, pleading for strength wherewith to work.

We sustain a loss when we neglect the privilege of associating together to strengthen and encourage one another in the service of God. The truths of His Word lose their vividness and importance in our minds. Our hearts cease to be enlightened and aroused by their sanctifying influence, and we decline in spirituality. In our association as Christians we lose much by lack of sympathy with one another. **He who shuts himself up to himself is not filling the position that God designed he should.** The proper cultivation of the social elements in our nature brings us into sympathy with others and is a means of development and strength to us in the service of God.

If Christians would associate together, speaking to each other of the love of God and of the precious truths of redemption, their own hearts would be refreshed and they would refresh one another. **We may be daily learning more of our heavenly Father, gaining a fresh experience of His grace; then we shall desire to speak of His love; and as we do this, our own hearts will be warmed and encouraged. If we thought and talked more of Jesus, and less of self, we should have far more of His presence.**

If we would but think of God as often as we have evidence of His care for us we should keep Him ever in our thoughts and should delight to talk of Him and to praise Him. We talk of temporal things because we have an interest in them. We talk of our friends because we love them; our joys and our sorrows are bound up with them. Yet we have infinitely greater reason to love God than to love our earthly friends; it should be the most natural thing in the world to make Him first in all our thoughts, to talk of His goodness, and tell of His power. The rich gifts He has bestowed upon us were not intended to absorb our thoughts and love so much that we should have nothing to give to God; they are constantly to remind us of Him and to bind us in bonds of love and gratitude to our heavenly Benefactor. **We dwell too near the lowlands of earth. Let us raise our eyes to the open door of the Sanctuary above, where the light of the glory of God shines in the face of Christ**, who "is able also to save them to the uttermost that come unto God by Him" (Hebrews 7:25).

We need to praise God more "for His goodness, and for His wonderful works to the children of men!" Psalm 107:8. Our devotional exercises should not consist wholly in asking and receiving. **Let us not be always thinking of our wants and never of the benefits we receive. We do not pray any too much, but we are too sparing of giving thanks.** We are the constant recipients of God's mercies, and yet how little gratitude we express, how little we praise Him for what He has done for us.

Anciently the Lord bade Israel, when they met together for His service, "Ye shall eat before the Lord your God, and ye shall rejoice in all that ye put your hand unto, ye and your households, wherein the Lord thy God hath blessed thee" (Deuteronomy 12:7). **That which is done for the glory of God should be done with cheerfulness, with songs of praise and thanksgiving, not with sadness and gloom.**

Our God is a tender, merciful Father. His service should not be looked upon as a heart-saddening, distressing exercise. It should be a pleasure to worship the Lord and to take part in His work. God would not have His children, for whom so great salvation has been provided, act as if He were a hard, exacting taskmaster. He is their best Friend; and when they worship Him, He expects to be with them, to bless and comfort them, filling their hearts with joy and love. **The Lord desires**

His children to take comfort in His service and to find more pleasure than hardship in His work. **He desires that those who come to worship Him shall carry away with them precious thoughts of His care and love,** that they may be cheered in all the employments of daily life, that they may have grace to deal honestly and faithfully in all things.

We must gather about the cross. Christ and Him crucified should be the theme of contemplation, of conversation, and of our most joyful emotion. We should keep in our thoughts every blessing we receive from God, and when we realize His great love we should be willing to trust everything to the hand that was nailed to the cross for us.

The soul may ascend nearer heaven on the wings of praise. God is worshiped with song and music in the courts above, and as we express our gratitude we are approximating to the worship of the heavenly hosts. "Whoso offereth praise glorifieth" God (Psalm 50:23). **Let us with reverent joy come before our Creator, with "thanksgiving, and the voice of melody"** (Isaiah 51:3).

What to Do with Doubt

Many, especially those who are young in the Christian life, are at times troubled with the suggestions of skepticism. There are in the Bible many things which they cannot explain, or even understand, and Satan employs these to shake their faith in the Scriptures as a revelation from God. They ask, "How shall I know the right way? If the Bible is indeed the Word of God, how can I be freed from these doubts and perplexities?"

God never asks us to believe, without giving suffi-

cient evidence upon which to base our faith. His existence, His character, the truthfulness of His Word, are all established by testimony that appeals to our reason; and this testimony is abundant. **Yet God has never removed the possibility of doubt.** Our faith must rest upon evidence, not demonstration. **Those who wish to doubt will have opportunity; while those who really desire to know the truth will find plenty of evidence on which to rest their faith.**

It is impossible for finite minds fully to comprehend the character or the works of the Infinite One. To the keenest intellect, the most highly educated mind, **that holy Being must ever remain clothed in mystery.** "Canst thou by searching find out God? canst thou find out the Almighty unto perfection? It is as high as heaven; what canst thou do? deeper than hell; what canst thou know?" Job 11:7-8.

The apostle Paul exclaims, "O the depth of the riches both of the wisdom and knowledge of God! how unsearchable are His judgments, and His ways past finding out!" Romans 11:33. But though "clouds and darkness are round about Him . . righteousness and judgment are the foundation of His throne" (Psalm 97:2, R.V.). **We can so far comprehend His dealings with us, and the motives by which He is actuated, that we may discern boundless love and mercy united to infinite power. We can understand as much of His purposes as it is for our good to know**; and beyond this we must still trust the hand that is omnipotent, the heart that is full of love.

The Word of God, like the character of its divine Author, presents mysteries that can never be fully comprehended by finite beings. The entrance of sin into the world, the Incarnation of Christ, regeneration, the resurrection, and many other subjects presented in the Bible, are mysteries too deep for the human mind to explain, or even fully to comprehend. **But we have no reason to doubt God's Word because we cannot understand the mysteries of His providence. In the natural world we are constantly surrounded with mysteries that we cannot fathom.** The very humblest forms of life present a problem that the wisest of philosophers is powerless to explain. Everywhere are wonders beyond our ken. Should we then be surprised to find that in the spiritual world also there are mysteries that we cannot fathom? **The difficulty lies solely in the weakness and narrowness of the human mind.** God has given us in the Scriptures sufficient evidence of their divine character, and **we are not to doubt His Word because we cannot understand all the mysteries of His providence.**

The apostle Peter says that there are in Scripture "things hard to be understood, which they that are unlearned and unstable wrest . . unto their own destruction" (2 Peter 3:16). **The difficulties of Scripture have been urged by skeptics as an argument against the Bible; but so far from this, they constitute a strong evidence of its divine inspiration.** If it contained no account of God but that which we could easily comprehend; if His greatness and majesty could be grasped by finite minds, then the Bible would not bear the unmistakable credentials of divine authority. **The very grandeur and mystery of the themes presented should inspire faith in it as the Word of God.**

The Bible unfolds truth with a simplicity and a perfect adaptation to the needs and longings of the human heart, that has astonished and charmed the most highly cultivated minds, while it enables the humble and uncultured to discern the way of salvation. **And yet these simply stated truths lay hold upon subjects so elevated, so far-reaching, so infinitely beyond the power of human comprehension, that we can accept**

them only because God has declared them. Thus the plan of redemption is laid open to us, so that **every soul may see the steps he is to take in repentance toward God and faith toward our Lord Jesus Christ, in order to be saved in God's appointed way**; yet beneath these truths, so easily understood, lie mysteries that are the hiding of His glory—mysteries that overpower the mind in its research, yet inspire the sincere seeker for truth with reverence and faith. **The more he searches the Bible, the deeper is his conviction that it is the Word of the living God, and human reason bows before the majesty of divine revelation.**

To acknowledge that we cannot fully comprehend the great truths of the Bible is only to admit that the finite mind is inadequate to grasp the infinite; that man, with his limited, human knowledge, cannot understand the purposes of Omniscience.

Because they cannot fathom all its mysteries, the skeptic and the infidel reject God's Word; and not all who profess to believe the Bible are free from danger on this point. The apostle says, "Take heed, brethren, lest there be in any of you an evil heart of unbelief, in departing from the living God." Hebrews 3:12. **It is right to study closely the teachings of the Bible and to search into "the deep things of God" so far as they are revealed in Scripture** (1 Corinthians 2:10). While "the secret things belong unto the Lord our God . . those things which are revealed belong unto us." Deuteronomy 29:29. **But it is Satan's work to pervert the investigative powers of the mind.** A certain pride is mingled with the consideration of Bible truth, so that men feel impatient and defeated if they cannot explain every portion of Scripture to their satisfaction. It is too humiliating to them to acknowledge that they do not understand the inspired words. **They are unwilling to wait patiently**

until God shall see fit to reveal the truth to them. They feel that their unaided human wisdom is sufficient to enable them to comprehend the Scripture, and failing to do this, they virtually deny its authority. It is true that many theories and doctrines popularly supposed to be derived from the Bible have no foundation in its teaching, and indeed are contrary to the whole tenor of inspiration. These things have been a cause of doubt and perplexity to many minds. They are not, however, chargeable to God's Word, but to man's perversion of it.

If it were possible for created beings to attain to a full understanding of God and His works, then, having reached this point, there would be for them no further discovery of truth, no growth in knowledge, no further development of mind or heart. God would no longer be supreme; and man, having reached the limit of knowledge and attainment, would cease to advance. Let us thank God that it is not so. God is infinite; in Him are "all the treasures of wisdom and knowledge" (Colossians 2:3). **And to all eternity men may be ever searching, ever learning, and yet never exhaust the treasures of His wisdom, His goodness, and His power.**

God intends that even in this life the truths of His Word shall be ever unfolding to His people. There is only one way in which this knowledge can be obtained. **We can attain to an understanding of God's Word only through the illumination of that Spirit by which the Word was given.** "The things of God knoweth no man, but the Spirit of God"; "for the Spirit searcheth all things, yea, the deep things of God." 1 Corinthians 2:11, 10. And the Saviour's promise to His followers was, "When He, the Spirit of truth, is come, He will guide you into all truth . . For He shall receive of Mine, and shall show it unto you." John 16:13-14.

God desires man to exercise his reasoning pow-

ers; and the study of the Bible will strengthen and
elevate the mind as no other study can. Yet we are to
beware of deifying reason, which is subject to the weakness and infirmity of humanity. If we would not have
the Scriptures clouded to our understanding, so that
the plainest truths shall not be comprehended, **we must
have the simplicity and faith of a little child, ready to
learn, and beseeching the aid of the Holy Spirit.** A
sense of the power and wisdom of God, and of our inability to comprehend His greatness, should inspire us
with humility, and **we should open His Word, as we
would enter His presence, with holy awe. When we
come to the Bible, reason must acknowledge an authority superior to itself, and heart and intellect must
bow to the great I AM.**

There are many things apparently difficult or obscure, which God will make plain and simple to those
who thus seek an understanding of them. **But, without
the guidance of the Holy Spirit, we shall be continually liable to wrest the Scriptures or to misinterpret
them.** There is much reading of the Bible that is without
profit and in many cases a positive injury. **When the
Word of God is opened without reverence and without prayer; when the thoughts and affections are not
fixed upon God, or in harmony with His will, the mind
is clouded with doubt**; and in the very study of the Bible,
skepticism strengthens. **The enemy takes control of
the thoughts, and he suggests interpretations that are
not correct.** Whenever men are not in word and deed
seeking to be in harmony with God, then, however learned
they may be, they are liable to err in their understanding
of Scripture, and it is not safe to trust to their explanations. **Those who look to the Scriptures to find discrepancies, have not spiritual insight.** With distorted
vision they will see many causes for doubt and unbelief

in things that are really plain and simple.

Disguise it as they may, the real cause of doubt and skepticism, in most cases, is the love of sin. The teachings and restrictions of God's Word are not welcome to the proud, sin-loving heart, and those who are unwilling to obey its requirements are ready to doubt its authority. **In order to arrive at truth, we must have a sincere desire to know the truth and a willingness of heart to obey it.** And all who come in this spirit to the study of the Bible will find abundant evidence that it is God's Word, and they may gain an understanding of its truths that will make them wise unto salvation.

Christ has said, "If any man willeth to do His will, he shall know of the teaching." John 7:17, R.V. **Instead of questioning and caviling concerning that which you do not understand, give heed to the light that already shines upon you, and you will receive greater light.** By the grace of Christ, perform every duty that has been made plain to your understanding, and you will be enabled to understand and perform those of which you are now in doubt.

There is an evidence that is open to all,—the most highly educated, and the most illiterate,—the evidence of experience. God invites us to prove for ourselves the reality of His Word, the truth of His promises. He bids us "taste and see that the Lord is good" (Psalm 34:8). Instead of depending upon the word of another, we are to taste for ourselves. He declares, "Ask, and ye shall receive." John 16:24. **His promises will be fulfilled. They have never failed; they never can fail. And as we draw near to Jesus, and rejoice in the fullness of His love, our doubt and darkness will disappear in the light of His presence.**

The apostle Paul says that God "hath delivered us from the power of darkness, and hath translated us into the kingdom of His dear Son" (Colossians 1:13). **And everyone who has passed from death unto life is able to "set to his seal that God is true"** (John 3:33). **He can testify, "I needed help, and I found it in Jesus. Every want was supplied, the hunger of my soul was satisfied; and now the Bible is to me the revelation of Jesus Christ.** Do you ask why I believe in Jesus? Because He is to me a divine Saviour. Why do I believe the Bible? Because I have found it to be the voice of God to my soul." **We may have the witness in ourselves that the Bible is true, that Christ is the Son of God.** We know that we are not following cunningly devised fables.

Peter exhorts his brethren to "grow in grace, and in the knowledge of our Lord and Saviour Jesus Christ" (2 Peter 3:18). **When the people of God are growing in grace, they will be constantly obtaining a clearer understanding of His Word. They will discern new light and beauty in its sacred truths.** This has been true in the history of the church in all ages, and thus it will continue to the end. "The path of the righteous is as the light of dawn, that shineth more and more unto the perfect day." Proverbs 4:18, R.V., margin.

By faith we may look to the hereafter and grasp the pledge of God for a growth of intellect, the human faculties uniting with the divine, and every power of the soul being brought into direct contact with the Source of light. **We may rejoice that all which has perplexed us in the providences of God will then be made plain, things hard to be understood will then find an explanation; and where our finite minds discovered only confusion and broken purposes, we shall see the most perfect and beautiful harmony.** "Now we see through a glass, darkly; but then face to face: now I know in part; but then shall I know even as also I am known." 1 Corinthians 13:12.

Rejoicing in the Lord

The children of God are called to be representatives of Christ, showing forth the goodness and mercy of the Lord. As Jesus has revealed to us the true character of the Father, so we are to reveal Christ to a world that does not know His tender, pitying love. "As Thou hast sent Me into the world," said Jesus, "even so have I also sent them into the world." "I in them, and Thou in Me . . that the world may know that Thou hast sent Me." John 17: 18, 23. The apostle Paul says to the disciples of Jesus, "Ye are manifestly declared to be the epistle of Christ," "known and read of all men." 2 Corinthians 3:3, 2. **In every one of His children, Jesus sends a letter to the world. If you are Christ's follower, He sends in you a letter to the family, the village, the street, where you live.** Jesus, dwelling in you, desires to speak to the hearts of those who are not acquainted with Him. Perhaps they do not read the Bible, or do not hear the voice that speaks to them in its pages; they do not see the love of God through His works. But if you are a true representative of Jesus, it may be that through you they will be led to understand something of His goodness and be won to love and serve Him.

Christians are set as light bearers on the way to heaven. They are to reflect to the world the light shining upon them from Christ. Their life and character should be such that through them others will get a right conception of Christ and of His service.

If we do represent Christ, we shall make His service appear attractive, as it really is. Christians who gather up gloom and sadness to their souls, and mur-

mur and complain, are giving to others a false representation of God and the Christian life. They give the impression that God is not pleased to have His children happy, and in this they bear false witness against our heavenly Father.

Satan is exultant when he can lead the children of God into unbelief and despondency. He delights to see us mistrusting God, doubting His willingness and power to save us. He loves to have us feel that the Lord will do us harm by His providences. It is the work of Satan to represent the Lord as lacking in compassion and pity. He misstates the truth in regard to Him. He fills the imagination with false ideas concerning God; and instead of dwelling upon the truth in regard to our heavenly Father, we too often fix our minds upon the misrepresentations of Satan and dishonor God by distrusting Him and murmuring against Him. **Satan ever seeks to make the religious life one of gloom. He desires it to appear toilsome and difficult; and when the Christian presents in his own life this view of religion, he is, through his unbelief, seconding the falsehood of Satan.**

Many, walking along the path of life, dwell upon their mistakes and failures and disappointments, and their hearts are filled with grief and discouragement. While I was in Europe, a sister who had been doing this, and who was in deep distress, wrote to me, asking for some word of encouragement. The night after I had read her letter I dreamed that I was in a garden, and one who seemed to be the owner of the garden was conducting me through its paths. I was gathering the flowers and enjoying their fragrance, when this sister, who had been walking by my side, called my attention to some unsightly briers that were impeding her way. There she was mourning and grieving. She was not walking in the pathway, following the guide, but was walking among the briers and thorns. "Oh," she mourned, "is it not a pity that this beautiful garden is spoiled with thorns?" Then the guide said, "Let the thorns alone, for they will only wound you. Gather the roses, the lilies, and the pinks."

Have there not been some bright spots in your experience? Have you not had some precious seasons when your heart throbbed with joy in response to the Spirit of God? When you look back into the chapters of your life experience do you not find some pleasant pages? **Are not God's promises, like the fragrant flowers, growing beside your path on every hand? Will you not let their beauty and sweetness fill your heart with joy?**

The briers and thorns will only wound and grieve you; and if you gather only these things, and present them to others, are you not, besides slighting the goodness of God yourself, preventing those around you from walking in the path of life?

It is not wise to gather together all the unpleasant recollections of a past life,—its iniquities and disappointments,—to talk over them and mourn over them until we are overwhelmed with discouragement. A discouraged soul is filled with darkness, shutting out the light of God from his own soul and casting a shadow upon the pathway of others.

Thank God for the bright pictures which He has presented to us. Let us group together the blessed assurances of His love, that we may look upon them continually: The Son of God leaving His Father's throne, clothing His divinity with humanity, that He might rescue man from the power of Satan; His triumph in our behalf, opening heaven to men, revealing to human vision the presence chamber where the Deity unveils His glory; the fallen race uplifted from the pit of ruin into which sin had plunged it, and brought again into connection with the infinite God, and having endured the divine test through faith in our Redeemer, clothed in the righteousness of Christ, and exalted to His throne—these are the pictures which God would have us contemplate.

When we seem to doubt God's love and distrust His promises we dishonor Him and grieve His Holy Spirit. How would a mother feel if her children were constantly complaining of her, just as though she did not mean them well, when her whole life's effort had been to forward their interests and to give them comfort? Suppose they should doubt her love; it would break her heart. How would any parent feel to be thus treated by his children? **And how can our heavenly Father regard us when we distrust His love, which has led Him to give His only begotten Son that we might have life?** The apostle writes, "He that spared not His own Son, but delivered Him up for us all, how shall He not with Him also freely give us all things?" Romans 8:32. **And yet how many, by their actions, if not in word, are saying, "The Lord does not mean this for me. Perhaps He loves others, but He does not love me."**

All this is harming your own soul; for every word of doubt you utter is inviting Satan's temptations; it is strengthening in you the tendency to doubt, and it is grieving from you the ministering angels. **When Satan tempts you, breathe not a word of doubt or darkness.** If you choose to open the door to his suggestions, your mind will be filled with distrust and rebellious questioning. **If you talk out your feelings, every doubt you express not only reacts upon yourself, but it is a seed that will germinate and bear fruit in the life of others**, and it may be impossible to counteract the influence of your words. You yourself may be able to recover from the season of temptation and from the snare of Satan, but others who have been swayed by your influence may not be able to escape from the unbelief you have suggested. **How important that we speak only those things that will give spiritual strength and life!**

Angels are listening to hear what kind of report you are bearing to the world about your heavenly Master. Let your conversation be of Him who liveth to make intercession for you before the Father. **When you take the hand of a friend, let praise to God be on your lips and in your heart. This will attract his thoughts to Jesus.**

All have trials; griefs hard to bear, temptations hard to resist. Do not tell your troubles to your fellow mortals, but carry everything to God in prayer. Make it a rule never to utter one word of doubt or discouragement. You can do much to brighten the life of others and strengthen their efforts, by words of hope and holy cheer.

There is many a brave soul sorely pressed by temptation, almost ready to faint in the conflict with self and with the powers of evil. Do not discourage such a one in his hard struggle. **Cheer him with brave, hopeful words that shall urge him on his way.** Thus the light of Christ may shine from you. "None of us liveth to himself." Romans 14:7. **By our unconscious influence others may be encouraged and strengthened**, or they may be discouraged, and repelled from Christ and the truth.

There are many who have an erroneous idea of the life and character of Christ. They think that He was devoid of warmth and sunniness, that He was stern, severe, and joyless. In many cases the whole religious experience is colored by these gloomy views.

It is often said that Jesus wept, but that He was never known to smile. Our Saviour was indeed a Man of Sorrows, and acquainted with grief, for He opened His heart to all the woes of men. But though His life was self-denying and shadowed with pain and care, His spirit was not crushed. **His countenance did not wear an expression of grief and repining, but ever one of peaceful serenity. His heart was a wellspring of life, and wherever He went He carried rest and peace, joy and gladness.**

Our Saviour was deeply serious and intensely in earnest, but never gloomy or morose. **The life of those who imitate Him will be full of earnest purpose; they will have a deep sense of personal responsibility.** Levity will be repressed; there will be no boisterous merriment, no rude jesting; but the religion of Jesus gives peace like a river. It does not quench the light of joy; it does not restrain cheerfulness nor cloud the sunny, smiling face. **Christ came not to be ministered unto but to minister; and when His love reigns in the heart, we shall follow His example.**

If we keep uppermost in our minds the unkind and unjust acts of others we shall find it impossible to love them as Christ has loved us; but if our thoughts dwell upon the wondrous love and pity of Christ for us, the same spirit will flow out to others. We should love and respect one another, notwithstanding the faults and imperfections that we cannot help seeing. **Humility and self-distrust should be cultivated, and a patient tenderness with the faults of others.** This will kill out all narrowing selfishness and make us large-hearted and generous.

The psalmist says, **"Trust in the Lord, and do good**; so shalt thou dwell in the land, and verily thou shalt be fed." Psalm 37:3. "Trust in the Lord." Each day has its burdens, its cares and perplexities; and, when we meet how ready we are to talk of our difficulties and trials. So many borrowed troubles intrude, so many fears are indulged, such a weight of anxiety is expressed, that one might suppose we had no pitying, loving Saviour ready to hear all our requests and to be to us a present help in every time of need.

Some are always fearing, and borrowing trouble. Every day they are surrounded with the tokens of God's love; **every day they are enjoying the bounties of His providence; but they overlook these present blessings. Their minds are continually dwelling upon something disagreeable** which they fear may come; or some difficulty may really exist which, though small, blinds their eyes to the many things that demand gratitude. **The difficulties they encounter, instead of driving them to God, the only source of their help, separate them from Him because they awaken unrest and repining.**

Do we well to be thus unbelieving? Why should we be ungrateful and distrustful? Jesus is our friend; all heaven is interested in our welfare. We should not allow the perplexities and worries of everyday life to fret the mind and cloud the brow. If we do we shall always have something to vex and annoy. We should not indulge a solicitude that only frets and wears us, but does not help us to bear trials.

You may be perplexed in business; your prospects may grow darker and darker, and you may be threatened with loss; but do not become discouraged; cast your care upon God, and remain calm and cheerful. Pray for wisdom to manage your affairs with discretion, and thus prevent loss and disaster. **Do all you can on your part to bring about favorable results. Jesus has promised His aid, but not apart from our effort.** When, relying upon our Helper, you have done all you can, accept the result cheerfully.

It is not the will of God that His people should be weighed down with care. But our Lord does not deceive us. He does not say to us, "Do not fear; there are no dangers in your path." **He knows there are trials and**

dangers, and He deals with us plainly. He does not propose to take His people out of a world of sin and evil, but He points them to a never-failing refuge. His prayer for His disciples was, "I pray not that Thou shouldest take them out of the world, but that Thou shouldest keep them from the evil" John 17:15. "In the world," He says, "ye shall have tribulation: but be of good cheer; I have overcome the world" (John 16:33).

In His Sermon on the Mount, Christ taught His disciples precious lessons in regard to the necessity of trusting in God. These lessons were designed to encourage the children of God through all ages, and they have come down to our time full of instruction and comfort. The Saviour pointed His followers to the birds of the air as they warbled their carols of praise, unencumbered with thoughts of care, for "they sow not, neither do they reap." And yet the great Father provides for their needs. The Saviour asks, "Are ye not much better than they?" Matthew 6:26. **The great Provider for man and beast opens His hand and supplies all His creatures. The birds of the air are not beneath His notice. He does not drop the food into their bills, but He makes provision for their needs.** They must gather the grains He has scattered for them. They must prepare the material for their little nests. They must feed their young. They go forth singing to their labor, for "your heavenly Father feedeth them." And "are ye not much better than they?" Are not you, as intelligent, spiritual worshipers, of more value than the birds of the air? **Will not the Author of our being, the Preserver of our life, the One who formed us in His own divine image, provide for our necessities if we but trust in Him?**

Christ pointed His disciples to the flowers of the field, growing in rich profusion and glowing in the simple beauty which the heavenly Father had given

them, as an expression of His love to man. He said, "Consider the lilies of the field, how they grow." The beauty and simplicity of these natural flowers far outrival the splendor of Solomon. The most gorgeous attire produced by the skill of art cannot bear comparison with the natural grace and radiant beauty of the flowers of God's creation. Jesus asks, "If God so clothe the grass of the field, which today is, and tomorrow is cast into the oven, shall He not much more clothe you, O ye of little faith?" Matthew 6:30. If God, the divine Artist, gives to the simple flowers that perish in a day their delicate and varied colors, how much greater care will He have for those who are created in His own image? This lesson of Christ's is a rebuke to the anxious thought, the perplexity and doubt, of the faithless heart.

The Lord would have all His sons and daughters happy, peaceful, and obedient. Jesus says, **"My peace I give unto you: not as the world giveth, give I unto you. Let not your heart be troubled, neither let it be afraid."** John 14:27. "These things have I spoken unto you, that My joy might remain in you, and that your joy might be full." John 15:11.

Happiness that is sought from selfish motives, outside of the path of duty, is ill-balanced, fitful, and transitory; it passes away, and the soul is filled with loneliness and sorrow; **but there is joy and satisfaction in the service of God; the Christian is not left to walk in uncertain paths**; he is not left to vain regrets and disappointments. **If we do not have the pleasures of this life we may still be joyful in looking to the life beyond.**

But even here Christians may have the joy of communion with Christ; they may have the light of His love, the perpetual comfort of His presence. **Every step in life may bring us closer to Jesus, may give us a deeper experience of His love**, and may bring us one step nearer to the blessed home of peace. **Then let us not cast away our confidence, but have firm assurance, firmer than ever before.** "Hitherto hath the Lord helped us," (1 Samuel 7:12) and He will help us to the end. Let us look to the monumental pillars, reminders of what the Lord has done to comfort us and to save us from the hand of the destroyer. **Let us keep fresh in our memory all the tender mercies that God has shown us**,—the tears He has wiped away, the pains He has soothed, the anxieties removed, the fears dispelled, the wants supplied, the blessings bestowed,—thus strengthening ourselves for all that is before us through the remainder of our pilgrimage.

We cannot but look forward to new perplexities in the coming conflict, but we may look on what is past as well as on what is to come, and say, "Hitherto hath the Lord helped us." "As thy days, so shall thy strength be." Deuteronomy 33:25. The trial will not exceed the strength that shall be given us to bear it. Then let us take up our work just where we find it, believing that whatever may come, strength proportionate to the trial will be given.

And by and by the gates of heaven will be thrown open to admit God's children, and from the lips of the King of glory the benediction will fall on their ears like richest music, "Come, ye blessed of My Father, inherit the kingdom prepared for you from the foundation of the world." Matthew 25:34.

Then the redeemed will be welcomed to the home that Jesus is preparing for them. There their companions will not be the vile of earth, liars, idolaters, the impure, and unbelieving; but **they will associate with those who have overcome Satan and through divine grace have formed perfect characters. Every sinful tendency, every imperfection, that afflicts them here**

has been removed by the blood of Christ, and the excellence and brightness of His glory, far exceeding the brightness of the sun, is imparted to them. And the moral beauty, the perfection of His character, shines through them, in worth far exceeding this outward splendor. **They are without fault before the great white throne, sharing the dignity and the privileges of the angels.**

In view of the glorious inheritance that may be his, "what shall a man give in exchange for his soul?" (Matthew 16:26). He may be poor, yet he possesses in himself a wealth and dignity that the world could never bestow. **The soul redeemed and cleansed from sin, with all its noble powers, dedicated to the service of God, is of surpassing worth**; and there is joy in heaven in the presence of God and the holy angels over one soul redeemed, a joy that is expressed in songs of holy triumph.

This is the end of the book, Steps to Christ.

"**Soon we shall witness the coronation of our King.** Those whose lives have been hidden with Christ, those who on this earth have fought the good fight of faith, will shine forth with the Redeemer's glory in the kingdom of God.

It will not be long till we shall see Him in whom our hopes of eternal life are centered. And in His presence, all the trials and sufferings of this life will be as nothingness

"**Look up, look up, and let your faith continually increase. Let this faith guide you along the narrow path that leads through the gates of the city of God into the great beyond, the wide, unbounded future of glory that is for the redeemed.**"
—*9 Testimonies, 287-288*

The Origin of Evil

How DID evil begin? Why IS there sin anyway? Here is the as-
tounding story of what happened. For this is the story of how sin
began—and how it will end.

Although surrounded by continual selflessness, something hap-
pened. What could turn an angel of light into a devil—and do it right
in the middle of heaven? This is something you will want to read. It
will tell you why God had to wait—and the wonderful future in store for
His children—because He did —

To many minds, the origin of sin and the reason
for its existence are a source of great perplexity. They
see the work of evil, with its terrible results of woe
and desolation, and they question how all this can
exist under the sovereignty of One who is infinite in
wisdom, in power, and in love. Here is a mystery, of
which they find no explanation. And in their uncertainty and doubt, they are blinded to truths plainly revealed in God's Word, and essential to salvation. There
are those who, in their inquiries concerning the existence of sin, endeavor to search into that which God has
never revealed; hence they find no solution of their difficulties; and such as are actuated by a disposition to
doubt and cavil, seize upon this as an excuse for reject-
ing the words of Holy Writ. Others, however, fail of a
satisfactory understanding of the great problem of evil,
from the fact that tradition and misinterpretation have
obscured the teaching of the Bible concerning the char-

acter of God, the nature of His government, and the principles of His dealing with sin.

It is impossible to so explain the origin of sin as to give a reason for its existence. Yet enough may be understood concerning both the origin and the final disposition of sin, to fully make manifest the justice and benevolence of God in all His dealings with evil. Nothing is more plainly taught in Scripture than that **God was in nowise responsible for the entrance of sin**; that there was no arbitrary withdrawal of divine grace, no deficiency in the divine government, that gave occasion for the uprising of rebellion. **Sin is an intruder, for whose presence no reason can be given. It is mysterious, unaccountable; to excuse it, is to defend it.** Could excuse for it be found, or cause be shown for its existence, it would cease to be sin. **Our only definition of sin is that given in the Word of God; it is "the transgression of the law";** it is the outworking of a principle at war with the great law of love which is the foundation of the divine government.

Before the entrance of evil, there was peace and joy throughout the universe. All was in perfect harmony with the Creator's will. Love for God was supreme, love for one another impartial. Christ the Word, the only begotten of God, was one with the eternal Father,—one in nature, in character, and in purpose,—the only being in all the universe that could enter into all the counsels and purposes of God. By Christ, the Father wrought in the creation of all heavenly beings. "By him were all things created, that are in Heaven . . whether they be thrones, or dominions, or principalities, or powers" (Colossians 1:16); and to Christ, equally with the Father, all Heaven gave allegiance.

The law of love being the foundation of the government of God, the happiness of all created beings depended upon their perfect accord with its great principles of righteousness. **God desires from all His creatures the service of love,—homage that springs from an intelligent appreciation of His character. He takes no pleasure in a forced allegiance**, and to all He grants freedom of will, that they may render Him voluntary service.

But there was one that chose to pervert this freedom. Sin originated with him, who, next to Christ, had been most honored of God, and who stood highest in power and glory among the inhabitants of Heaven. **Before his fall, Lucifer was first of the covering cherubs, holy and undefiled.** "Thus saith the Lord God: Thou sealest up the sum, full of wisdom, and perfect in beauty. Thou hast been in Eden the garden of God; every precious stone was thy covering." "Thou art the anointed cherub that covereth; and I have set thee so; thou wast upon the holy mountain of God; thou hast walked up and down in the midst of the stones of fire. Thou wast perfect in thy ways from the day that thou wast created, till iniquity was found in thee." Ezekiel 28:12-15.

Lucifer might have remained in favor with God, beloved and honored by all the angelic host, exercising his noble powers to bless others and to glorify His Maker. But, says the prophet, "Thine heart was lifted up because of thy beauty, thou hast corrupted thy wisdom by reason of thy brightness." Ezekiel 28:17. **Little by little, Lucifer came to indulge a desire for self-exaltation.** "Thou hast set thine heart as the heart of God." "Thou hast said . . I will exalt my throne above the stars of God; I will sit also upon the mount of the congregation." "I will ascend above the heights of the clouds; I will be like the Most High." Ezekiel 28:6; Isaiah 14:13, 14. **Instead of seeking to make God supreme in the affections and allegiance of His creatures, it was Lucifer's endeavor to win their service and homage to himself.**

And, coveting the honor which the infinite Father had bestowed upon His Son, this prince of angels aspired to power which it was the prerogative of Christ alone to wield.

All Heaven had rejoiced to reflect the Creator's glory and to show forth His praise. And while God was thus honored, all had been peace and gladness. But a note of discord now marred the celestial harmonies. The service and exaltation of self, contrary to the Creator's plan, awakened forebodings of evil in minds to whom God's glory was supreme. **The heavenly councils pleaded with Lucifer.** The Son of God presented before him the greatness, the goodness, and the justice of the Creator, and the sacred, unchanging nature of His law. God Himself had established the order of Heaven; and in departing from it, Lucifer would dishonor his Maker, and bring ruin upon himself. **But the warning, given in infinite love and mercy, only aroused a spirit of resistance. Lucifer allowed jealousy of Christ to prevail, and he became the more determined.**

Pride in his own glory nourished the desire for supremacy. The high honors conferred upon Lucifer were not appreciated as the gift of God, and called forth no gratitude to the Creator. He gloried in his brightness and exaltation, and aspired to be equal with God. He was beloved and reverenced by the heavenly host. Angels delighted to execute his commands, and he was clothed with wisdom and glory above them all. **Yet the Son of God was the acknowledged sovereign of Heaven, one in power and authority with the Father. In all the counsels of God, Christ was a participant, while Lucifer was not permitted thus to enter into the divine purposes.** "Why," questioned this mighty angel, "should Christ have the supremacy? Why is He thus honored above Lucifer?"

Leaving his place in the immediate presence of God, Lucifer went forth to diffuse the spirit of discontent among the angels. Working with mysterious secrecy, and for a time concealing his real purpose under an appearance of reverence for God, **he endeavored to excite dissatisfaction concerning the laws that governed heavenly beings, intimating that they imposed an unnecessary restraint.** Since their natures were holy, he urged that the angels should obey the dictates of their own will. He sought to create sympathy for himself, by representing that God had dealt unjustly with him in bestowing supreme honor upon Christ. **He claimed that in aspiring to greater power and honor he was not aiming at self-exaltation, but was seeking to secure liberty for all the inhabitants of Heaven, that by this means they might attain to a higher state of existence.**

God, in His great mercy, bore long with Lucifer. He was not immediately degraded from his exalted station when he first indulged the spirit of discontent, nor even when he began to present his false claims before the loyal angels. Long was he retained in Heaven. Again and again he was offered pardon, on condition of repentance and submission. **Such efforts as only infinite love and wisdom could devise, were made to convince him of his error. The spirit of discontent had never before been known in Heaven. Lucifer himself did not at first see whither he was drifting**; he did not understand the real nature of his feelings. **But as his dissatisfaction was proved to be without cause, Lucifer was convinced that he was in the wrong, that the divine claims were just, and that he ought to acknowledge them as such before all Heaven. Had he done this, he might have saved himself and many angels.** He had not at this time fully cast off his allegiance to God. Though he had forsaken his position as covering cherub, yet if he had been willing to return to God, acknowledging the Creator's wisdom, and satisfied to fill the place appointed him in God's great plan, he would have been re-instated in his office. **But pride forbade him to submit. He persistently defended his own course, maintained that he had no need of repentance, and fully committed himself, in the great controversy, against his Maker.**

All the powers of his master-mind were now bent to the work of deception, to secure the sympathy of the angels that had been under his command. Even the fact that Christ had warned and counseled him, was perverted to serve his traitorous designs. To those whose loving trust bound them most closely to him, Satan had represented that he was wrongly judged, that his position was not respected, and that his liberty was to be abridged. **From misrepresentation of the words of Christ, he passed to prevarication and direct falsehood**, accusing the Son of God of a design to humiliate him before the inhabitants of Heaven. He sought also to make a false issue between himself and the loyal angels. **All whom he could not subvert and bring fully to his side, he accused of indifference to the interests of heavenly beings. The very work which he himself was doing, he charged upon those who remained true to God.** And to sustain his charge of God's injustice toward him, he resorted to misrepresentation of the words and acts of the Creator. **It was his policy to perplex the angels with subtle arguments concerning the purposes of God. Everything that was simple he shrouded in mystery**, and by artful perversion cast doubt upon the plainest statements of Jehovah. His high position, in such close connection with the divine administration, gave greater force to his representations, and many were induced to unite with him in rebellion against Heaven's authority.

God in His wisdom permitted Satan to carry forward his work, until the spirit of disaffection ripened into active revolt. It was necessary for his plans to be fully developed, that their true nature and tendency might be seen by all. Lucifer, as the anointed cherub, had been highly exalted; he was greatly loved by the heavenly beings, and his influence over them was strong. God's government included not only the inhabitants of Heaven, but of all the worlds that he had created; and **Satan thought that if he could carry the angels of Heaven with him in rebellion, he could carry also the other worlds.** He had artfully presented his side of the question, employing sophistry and fraud to secure his objects. His power to deceive was very great, and by disguising himself in a cloak of falsehood he had gained an advantage. **Even the loyal angels could not fully discern his character, or see to what his work was leading.**

Satan had been so highly honored, and all his acts were so clothed with mystery, that it was difficult to disclose to the angels the true nature of his work. Until fully developed, sin would not appear the evil thing it was. Heretofore it had had no place in the universe of God, and holy beings had no conception of its nature and malignity. They could not discern the terrible consequences that would result from setting aside the divine law. **Satan had, at first, concealed his work under a specious profession of loyalty to God. He claimed to be seeking to promote the honor of God, the stability of His government, and the good of all the inhabitants of Heaven.** While instilling discontent into the minds of the angels under him, he had artfully made it appear that he was seeking to remove dissatisfaction. When he urged that changes be made in the order and laws of God's government, it was under the pretense that these were necessary in order to preserve harmony in Heaven.

In his dealing with sin, God could employ only righteousness and truth. Satan could use what God could not—flattery and deceit. He had sought to falsify the word of God, and had misrepresented His plan of government before the angels, claiming that God was not just in laying laws and rules upon the inhabitants of Heaven; that in requiring submission and obedience from His creatures, He was seeking merely the exaltation of himself. **Therefore it must be demonstrated before the inhabitants of Heaven as well as of all the worlds, that God's government was just, His law perfect.** Satan had made it appear that He Himself was seeking to promote the good of the universe. The true character of the usurper, and his real object, must be understood by all. He must have time to manifest himself by his wicked works.

The discord which his own course had caused in Heaven, Satan charged upon the law and government of God. All evil he declared to be the result of the divine administration. He claimed that it was his own object to improve upon the statutes of Jehovah. Therefore it was necessary that he should demonstrate the nature of His claims, and show the working out of his proposed changes in the divine law. **His own work must condemn him. Satan had claimed from the first that he was not in rebellion. The whole universe must see the deceiver unmasked.**

Even when it was decided that he could no longer remain in Heaven, infinite wisdom did not destroy Satan. Since the service of love can alone be acceptable to God, the allegiance of His creatures must rest upon a conviction of His justice and benevolence. **The inhabitants of Heaven and of other worlds, being unprepared**

to comprehend the nature or consequences of sin, could not then have seen the justice and mercy of God in the destruction of Satan. Had he been immediately blotted from existence, they would have served God from fear, rather than from love. The influence of the deceiver would not have been fully destroyed, nor would the spirit of rebellion have been utterly eradicated. **Evil must be permitted to come to maturity. For the good of the entire universe through ceaseless ages, Satan must more fully develop his principles**, that his charges against the divine government might be seen in their true light by all created beings, that the justice and mercy of God and the immutability of His law might forever be placed beyond all question.

Satan's rebellion was to be a lesson to the universe through all coming ages, a perpetual testimony to the nature and terrible results of sin. The working out of Satan's rule, its effects upon both men and angels, would show what must be the fruit of setting aside the divine authority. It would testify that with the existence of God's government and His law is bound up the well-being of all the creatures He has made. Thus the history of this terrible experiment of rebellion was to be a perpetual safeguard to all holy intelligences, to prevent them from being deceived as to the nature of transgression, to save them from committing sin, and suffering its punishment.

To the very close of the controversy in Heaven, the great usurper continued to justify himself. When it was announced that with all his sympathizers he must be expelled from the abodes of bliss, then the rebel leader boldly avowed his contempt for the Creator's law. He reiterated his claim that angels needed no control, but should be left to follow their own will, which would ever guide them right. **He denounced the**

divine statutes as a restriction of their liberty, and declared that it was his purpose to secure the abolition
of law; that, freed from this restraint, the hosts of Heaven
might enter upon a more exalted, more glorious state of
existence.

**With one accord, Satan and his host threw the
blame of their rebellion wholly upon Christ, declaring that if they had not been reproved, they would
never have rebelled.** Thus stubborn and defiant in their
disloyalty, seeking vainly to overthrow the government of
God, yet blasphemously claiming to be themselves the
innocent victims of oppressive power, **the arch-rebel and
all his sympathizers were at last banished from Heaven.**

**The same spirit that prompted rebellion in Heaven,
still inspires rebellion on earth. Satan has continued
with men the same policy which he pursued with the
angels.** His spirit now reigns in the children of disobedience. Like him they seek to break down the restraints of
the law of God, and promise men liberty through transgression of its precepts. Reproof of sin still arouses the
spirit of hatred and resistance. When God's messages of
warning are brought home to the conscience, **Satan leads
men to justify themselves, and to seek the sympathy
of others in their course of sin. Instead of correcting
their errors, they excite indignation against the re-
prover**, as if he were the sole cause of difficulty. From
the days of righteous Abel to our own time, such is the
spirit which has been displayed toward those who dare
to condemn sin.

By the same misrepresentation of the character of
God as he had practiced in Heaven, causing him to be
regarded as severe and tyrannical, **Satan induced man
to sin. And having succeeded thus far, he declared
that God's unjust restrictions had led to man's fall, as
they had led to his own rebellion.**

But the Eternal One Himself proclaims His character: "The Lord God, merciful and gracious, long-suffering, and abundant in goodness and truth, keeping mercy for thousands, forgiving iniquity and transgression and sin, and that will by no means clear the guilty." Exodus 34:6, 7.

In the banishment of Satan from Heaven, God declared His justice, and maintained the honor of His throne. But when man had sinned through yielding to the deceptions of this apostate spirit, God gave an evidence of His love by yielding up His only begotten Son to die for the fallen race. In the atonement the character of God is revealed. The mighty argument of the cross demonstrates to the whole universe that the course of sin which Lucifer had chosen was in nowise chargeable upon the government of God.

In the contest between Christ and Satan, during the Saviour's earthly ministry, the character of the great deceiver was unmasked. Nothing could so effectually have uprooted Satan from the affections of the heavenly angels and the whole loyal universe as did his cruel warfare upon the world's Redeemer. The daring blasphemy of his demand that Christ should pay him homage, his presumptuous boldness in bearing Him to the mountain summit and the pinnacle of the temple, the malicious intent betrayed in urging Him to cast Himself down from the dizzy height, the unsleeping malice that hunted Him from place to place, inspiring the hearts of priests and people to reject His love, and at the last to cry, "Crucify Him! crucify Him!"—all this excited the amazement and indignation of the universe.

It was Satan that prompted the world's rejection of Christ. The prince of evil exerted all his power and cunning to destroy Jesus; for he saw that the Saviour's mercy and love, His compassion and pitying tender-

ness, were representing to the world the character of God. Satan contested every claim put forth by the Son of God, and employed men as His agents to fill the Saviour's life with suffering and sorrow. The sophistry and falsehood by which he had sought to hinder the work of Jesus, the hatred manifested through the children of disobedience, his cruel accusations against Him whose life was one of unexampled goodness, all sprung from deep-seated revenge. **The pent-up fires of envy and malice, hatred and revenge, burst forth on Calvary against the Son of God, while all Heaven gazed upon the scene in silent horror.**

When the great sacrifice had been consummated, Christ ascended on high, refusing the adoration of angels until He had presented the request, "I will that they also, whom thou hast given Me, be with Me where I am." John 17:24. Then with inexpressible love and power came forth the answer from the Father's throne, "Let all the angels of God worship Him." Hebrews 1:6. Not a stain rested upon Jesus. His humiliation ended, His sacrifice completed, there was given unto Him a name that is above every name.

Now the guilt of Satan stood forth without excuse. He had revealed his true character as a liar and a murderer. It was seen that the very same spirit with which he ruled the children of men, who were under his power, he would have manifested had he been permitted to control the inhabitants of Heaven. **He had claimed that the transgression of God's law would bring liberty and exaltation; but it was seen to result in bondage and degradation.**

Satan's lying charges against the divine character and government appeared in their true light. He had accused God of seeking merely the exaltation of Himself in requiring submission and obedience from His creatures, and had declared that while the Creator exacted self-denial from all others, He Himself practiced no self-denial, made no sacrifice. **Now it was seen that for the salvation of a fallen and sinful race, the Ruler of the universe had made the greatest sacrifice which love could make**; for "God was in Christ, reconciling the world unto Himself." 2 Corinthians 5:19. It was seen, also, that while Lucifer had opened the door for the entrance of sin, by his desire for honor and supremacy, **Christ had, in order to destroy sin, humbled Himself, and become obedient unto death.**

God had manifested His abhorrence of the principles of rebellion. All Heaven saw His justice revealed, both in the condemnation of Satan and in the redemption of man. Lucifer had declared that if the law of God was changeless, and its penalty could not be remitted, every transgressor must be forever debarred from the Creator's favor. He had claimed that the sinful race were placed beyond redemption, and were therefore his rightful prey. **But the death of Christ was an argument in man's behalf that could not be overthrown.** The penalty of the law fell upon him who was equal with God, and man was free to accept the righteousness of Christ, and by a life of penitence and humiliation to triumph, as the Son of God had triumphed, over the power of Satan. Thus God is just, and yet the justifier of all who believe in Jesus.

But it was not merely to accomplish the redemption of man that Christ came to the earth to suffer and to die. He came to "magnify the law" and to "make it honorable." Not alone that the inhabitants of this world might regard the law as it should be regarded; but it was to demonstrate to all the worlds of the universe that God's law is unchangeable. **Could its claims have been set aside, then the Son of God need not have**

yielded up His life to atone for its transgression. **The death of Christ proves it immutable.** And the sacrifice to which infinite love impelled the Father and the Son, that sinners might be redeemed, demonstrates to all the universe—what nothing less than this plan of atonement could have sufficed to do—that justice and mercy are the foundation of the law and government of God.

In the final execution of the Judgment it will be seen that no cause for sin exists. When the Judge of all the earth shall demand of Satan, "Why hast thou rebelled against Me, and robbed me of the subjects of My kingdom?" the originator of evil can render no excuse. Every mouth will be stopped, and all the hosts of rebellion will be speechless.

The cross of Calvary, while it declares the law immutable, proclaims to the universe that the wages of sin is death. In the Saviour's expiring cry, "It is finished," the death-knell of Satan was rung. The great controversy which had been so long in progress was then decided, and the final eradication of evil was made certain. The Son of God passed through the portals of the tomb, that "through death He might destroy him that had the power of death, that is, the devil." Hebrews 2:14. Lucifer's desire for self-exaltation had led him to say, "I will exalt my throne above the stars of God . . I will be like the Most High." God declares, "I will bring thee to ashes upon the earth . . and never shalt thou be any more." Isaiah 14:13, 14; Ezekiel 28:18, 19. When **"the day cometh that shall burn as an oven," "all the proud, yea, and all that do wickedly, shall be stubble; and the day that cometh shall burn them up**, saith the Lord of hosts, that it shall leave them neither root nor branch." Malachi 4:1.

The whole universe will have become witnesses to the nature and results of sin. And its utter extermina-

tion, which in the beginning would have brought fear to angels and dishonor to God, will now vindicate His love and establish His honor before a universe of beings who delight to do His will, and in whose heart is His law. **Never will evil again be manifest.** Says the Word of God, "Affliction shall not rise up the second time." Nahum 1:9. The law of God, which Satan has reproached as the yoke of bondage, will be honored as the law of liberty. **A tested and proved creation will never again be turned from allegiance to Him whose character has been fully manifested before them as fathomless love and infinite wisdom.**

"**Christ has given us no promise of help in bearing today the burdens of tomorrow** . . His grace is bestowed daily, for the day's need . . **One day alone is ours, and during this day we are to live for God.** For this one day we are to place in the hand of Christ, in solemn service, all our purposes and plans, casting all our care upon Him, for He careth for us. 'I know the thoughts that I think toward you, saith the Lord, thoughts of peace, and not of evil, to give you an expected end.' 'In returning and rest shall ye be saved; in quietness and in confidence shall be your strength.' Jeremiah 29:11; Isaiah 30:15.

"**If you will seek the Lord and be converted every day; if you will of your own spiritual choice be free and joyous in God**; if with gladsome consent of heart to His gracious call you come wearing the yoke of Christ,—the yoke of obedience and service,—**all your murmurings will be stilled, all your difficulties will be removed, all the perplexing problems that now confront you will be solved.**"

—Mount of Blessing, 101

Entering Upon A Deeper Worship

FACT NUMBER ONE—The Sabbath was given to all mankind at the Creation of this world.

The seventh-day Sabbath was given to mankind on the seventh day of Creation Week.

"Thus the heavens and the earth were finished, and all the host of them. And on the seventh day God ended His work which He had made; and He rested on the seventh day from all His work which He had made.

"And God blessed the seventh day, and sanctified it: because that in it He had rested from all His work which God created and made."—*Genesis 2:1-3.*

God dedicated and set aside the Sabbath as a rest day—2,000 years before the first Jew. Abraham is considered by all to have been the first Jew. He lived about 2000 B.C. Biblical records indicate that the Creation of this world took place about 4000 B.C. So the Bible Sabbath is not Jewish! It is for mankind; it is for all the world.

"The Sabbath was made for man."—*Mark 2:27.*

FACT NUMBER TWO—The Sabbath is a memorial of Creation and our salvation.

First, it is a memorial of Creation.

"It is a sign between Me and the children of Israel for ever: for in six days the Lord made heaven and earth, and on the seventh day He rested, and was refreshed."—*Exodus 31:17.*

As a memorial of the Creation of this world, the Sabbath cannot pass away without first having this world pass away—and creating a new one! Our planet could not have a new or different Sabbath day, without having it first hurled into oblivion—and then a new planet created from nothing. But no such event has occurred.

Second, **the Sabbath is a symbol of our salvation.** When we keep it, we tell all the world that we belong to God and that we serve and obey Him. The seventh-day Sabbath is a sign of our conversion, sanctification, and salvation:

"Verily My Sabbaths ye shall keep: for it is a sign between Me and you throughout your generations; that ye may know that I am the Lord that doth sanctify you."—*Exodus 31:13.*

"Moreover also I gave them My Sabbaths to be a sign between Me and them, that they might know that I am the Lord that sanctify them."—*Ezekiel 20:12.*

"And hallow My Sabbaths; and they shall be a sign between Me and you, that ye may know that I am the Lord your God."—*Ezekiel 20:20.*

But what about Christ's resurrection? Nowhere in Scripture were we told to keep any day in honor of Christ's resurrection. To do so is unscriptural. On the contrary, to set aside the Creation and sanctification Sabbath of the Bible—for another day of the week—and excuse it by saying that we do so "in honor of Christ's resurrection"—is indeed to do a very daring thing. Who dare presume to set aside the Memorial of Creation and salvation for any reason! To knowingly do so, flies in the face of repeated, direct, Biblical commands by the God of heaven. To do so denies that He is our Creator and Redeemer.

If we abandon the Bible Sabbath and keep another day holy, in the Judgment what excuse can we offer? There is no Bible reason for keeping the first day of the week holy instead of the seventh day.

FACT NUMBER THREE—**The people of God kept the Bible Sabbath before the Ten Commandments were given at Mount Sinai.**

The Sabbath Truth was first given to our race in Eden before the fall of man. It was given before sin existed, and apart from it. It was given to every man to link him to his God. And if Adam needed the Sabbath, we need it all the more today.

God's people had it before Mount Sinai. Four chapters before the Ten Commandments were given on Mount Sinai, the God of heaven spoke in such a way that it is obvious that the seventh-day Sabbath was already well-known by the people of God—but not always well-kept: Read Exodus 16.

There are those who say that the seventh-day Sabbath was not commanded by God, nor kept by man before it was spoken from Mount Sinai in Exodus 20. But Genesis 2:1-3 and Exodus 16 prove otherwise.

FACT NUMBER FOUR—*Th*e seventh-day Sabbath Commandment lies in the very heart of the Moral Law of Ten Commandments.

"Remember The Sabbath day, to keep it holy.

"Six days shalt thou labour, and do all thy work. But the seventh day is the Sabbath of the Lord thy God: in it thou shalt not do any work, thou, nor thy son, nor thy daughter, thy manservant, nor thy maidservant, nor thy cattle, nor thy stranger that is within thy gates.

"For in six days the Lord made heaven and earth, the sea, and all that in them is, and rested the seventh day: wherefore the Lord blessed the Sabbath day, and hallowed it."—*Exodus 20:8-11.*

The Sabbath Commandment is part of the Moral Law of Ten Commandments. The Apostle James tells us that if we break any part of this law, we have broken it all (James 2:10-12). We cannot tear out the Fourth Commandment without setting aside all the others as well. They all stand together, because the God of Heaven put them all together.

We do not decide which day of the week is to be kept holy unto God; He alone is to do this. It is for Him to command; it is for us to obey.

Some say that Genesis 2:1-3 is not a command for man to keep the Sabbath, and therefore we do not obey it. But Exodus 16 and 20 clearly show that man *is* commanded to keep it holy. And who dare say that the Ten Commandments were only for the Jewish race? Are the rest of us permitted to lie, steal, cheat, and commit adultery? Are only the Hebrews to observe these ten moral principles?

The reason for the commandment is the Creation of this world:

"For in six days the Lord made heaven and earth." This is not something local, merely for a Semitic race;—it is a commandment for all in the entire world who shall bow down and worship their Creator in humble thankfulness for His plan to save them through the life and death of Jesus Christ. It was given at the Creation of this world, and was given to every man, woman, and child who shall live on this planet.

God wrote these Ten Commandments with His own finger (Ex 31:18; Deut 9:10). **He wrote them on the most enduring thing in the world**, and that is rock (Ex 31:18). And He wishes to write them also on our hearts.

"This is the covenant that I will make with them after those days, saith the Lord: I will put My laws into their hearts, and in their minds will I write them."—*Hebrews 10:16 (Heb 8:10; Jer 31:33).*

And, if we will let Him, through the New Covenant He will write His holy law upon our hearts. To have the Ten Commandments written on our hearts means two things: First, a willingness to obey them and, second, letting God enable us to do so by the grace of Jesus, His Son. Obedience to God's law is to become an integral part of our lives.

FACT NUMBER FIVE—The weekly seventh-day Sabbath is part of the Moral Law contained in the Ten Commandments. It will stand forever. The yearly sabbaths were part of the ceremonial laws that prefigured, or foreshadowed, the death and ministry of Christ.

These "shadow laws," such as Passover and the Wave Sheaf, which were a part of the ceremonial or sacrificial law, would not endure past the death of Christ.

"For the [ceremonial] law having a shadow of good things to come, and not the very image of the things, can never with those sacrifices which they offered year by year continually make the comers thereunto perfect. For then would they not have ceased to be offered? . . But in those sacrifices there is a remembrance again made of sins every year. For it is not possible that the blood of bulls and of goats should take away sins."—*Hebrews 10:1-4.*

These ceremonial laws were not written on rock, but were contained in ordinances, written on parchment. The rock was to endure, but the ordinances that foreshadowed the death of Christ were to pass away at His death. It is for this reason that we do not today observe the yearly sabbaths of the Passover and the Wave Sheaf.

"Blotting out the handwriting of ordinances that was against us, which was contrary to us, and took it out of the way, nailing it to His cross . . Let no man therefore judge you in meat, or in drink, or in respect of an holyday, or of the new moon, or of the sabbath days. Which are a shadow of things to come; but the body is of Christ."—*Colossians 2:14,16-17.*

In the Greek it says, "or of the sabbaths." **There is one weekly Sabbath; it comes down to us from the Creation of this world and will be kept in the New Earth** (Isa 66:22-23). **But the yearly sabbaths did not begin until Moses.** They foreshadowed and explained the coming death of Christ till it happened; and, at His death, they were nailed to His cross.

If the ordinances containing the yearly sabbaths had not been set aside at Calvary, we would need now to sacrifice animals on various occasions throughout the year. But we are not now to slay lambs; for Christ, our Passover Lamb, has been sacrificed for us.

"Behold the Lamb of God, which taketh away the sin of the world."—*John 1:29.*

"For even Christ our Passover is sacrificed for us."—*1 Corinthians 5:7.*

FACT NUMBER SIX—**Christ's disciples faithfully kept the Bible Sabbath, not Sunday.**

The disciples had been with Jesus for three and a half years, and had listened closely to His teachings. What they did at the time of His death on Calvary shows what He taught them. The sacred importance of the seventh-day Sabbath was of such concern to them that they would not even prepare the body of Jesus properly for burial on Friday, lest they transgress the Fourth Commandment.

"And now when the even was come, because it was the preparation, that is, the day before the Sabbath . . Mary Magdalene and Mary the mother of Joses beheld where He was laid.

"And when the Sabbath was past, Mary Magdalene, and Mary the mother of James, and Salome, had bought sweet spices, that they might come and anoint Him. And very early in the morning the first day of the week, they came unto the sepulchre at the rising of the sun. And they said among themselves, Who shall roll us away the stone from the door of the sepulchre?"—*Mark 15:42, 47-16:3.*

For more on this, read Luke 23:53-24:2.

FACT NUMBER SEVEN—According to the New Testament, the Apostles of Jesus always kept the Bible Sabbath.

The Apostles kept the Bible Sabbath. Read Acts 13:14; Acts 13:42; Acts 16:13; Acts 17:1-2.

Paul supported himself by tentmaking; and then on the Sabbath, he would preach the gospel.

"Because he was of the same craft, he abode with them, and wrought: for by their occupation, they were tentmakers . . And he reasoned in the synagogue every Sabbath, and persuaded the Jews and the Greeks . . He continued there a year and six months, teaching the Word of God among them."—*Acts 18:3, 4, 11.*

Paul's manner was the same as Christ's custom: to keep the Bible Sabbath (Acts 17:1-2; Luke 4:16).

Paul never taught that the Moral Law was, or could be, set aside. It will ever govern the conduct of mankind:

"Do we then make void the law through faith? God forbid: yea, we establish the law."—*Romans 3:31.*

"What shall we say then? Shall we continue in sin, that grace may abound? God forbid. How shall we, that are dead to sin, live any longer therein?"—*Romans 6:1-2.*

"What shall we say then? Is the law sin? God forbid. Nay, I had not known sin, but by the law: for I had not known lust, except the law had said, Thou shalt not covet."—*Romans 7:7.*

Paul clearly saw that the problem was that we needed to obey the law; there was nothing wrong with the requirements of the law

itself.

"Wherefore the law is holy, and the commandment holy, and just, and good."—*Romans 7:12.*

"Circumcision is nothing, and uncircumcision is nothing, but [that which is important is] the keeping of the commandments of God."—*1 Corinthians 7:19.*

The moral standard that governs mankind was not relaxed or destroyed by the death of Christ; for, indeed, it is through the merits of Christ's sacrifice that we can be empowered to keep that law.

"Thou shalt call His name Jesus, for He shall save His people from their sins."—*Matthew 1:21.*

Jesus saves us from our sins, not in our sins. And since sin is the breaking of the Ten Commandments, it is obvious that He saves us by enabling us, strengthening us, to keep that law.

"Whosoever committeth sin transgresseth also the law: for sin is the transgression of the law."—*1 John 3:4.*

The other Apostles saw this same great truth, that the moral standard that governs mankind was not relaxed or destroyed by the death of Christ:

"But be ye doers of the Word, and not hearers only, deceiving your own selves. For if any be a hearer of the Word, and not a doer, he is like unto a man beholding his natural face In a glass. For he beholdeth himself, and goeth his way, and straightway forgetteth what manner of man he was.

"But whoso looketh into the perfect law of liberty, and continueth therein, he being not a forgetful hearer, but a doer of the work, this man shall be blessed in his deed . . For whosoever shall keep the whole law, and yet offend in one point, he is guilty of all. For He that saith, Do not commit adultery, said also, Do not kill. Now if thou commit no adultery, yet if thou kill, thou art become a transgressor of the law. So speak ye, and so do, as they that shall be judged by the law of liberty . . Faith, if it hath not works, is dead, being alone. Yea, a man may say, Thou hast faith, and I have works; shew me thy faith without thy works, and I will shew thee my faith by my works."—*James 1:22-25;*

2:10-12, 17-18.

"By this we know that we love the children of God, when we love God, and keep His commandments. For this is the love of God, that we keep His commandments: and His commandments are not grievous."—*1 John 5:2-3.*

FACT NUMBER EIGHT—God predicted in Scripture that men would later try to change the Law of God—and especially the "time law."

The Bible Sabbath is very important—for it is the very center of our worship of God! If men were later to try to change it to another day, we should surely expect a Bible prophecy saying that it would happen.

"And he [the little horn power] shall speak great words against the most High, and shall wear out the saints of the most High, and think to change times and laws: and they shall be given into His hand until a time and times and the dividing of time."—*Daniel 7:25.*

The church of the Dark Ages was to rule the world for 1260 years, and during this time would try to tear out God's holy Time Law and put a counterfeit in its place. Oh, what blasphemy men can dream up, when they are tempted by Satan to gain religious control of their fellow men!

"For that day [the Second Coming of Christ] shall not come, except there come a falling away first, and that man of sin be revealed, the son of perdition; who opposeth and exalteth himself above all that is called God, or that is worshiped."—*2 Thessalonians 2:3-4.*

God said:

"And hallow My Sabbaths; and they shall be a sign between Me and you, that ye may know that I am the Lord your God." —*Ezekiel 20:20.*

After the New Testament was finished and the Apostles had died, men tried transfer the sacredness from the seventh to the first day of the week. They tried to change the "time law."

Roman Catholic: "It is well to remind the Presbyterians,

Baptists, Methodists, and all other Christians, that the Bible does not support them anywhere in their observance of Sunday. Sunday is an institution of the Roman Catholic Church, and those who observe the day observe a commandment of the Catholic Church."—*Priest Brady, in an address at Elizabeth, N.J., March 17, 1903; reported in the Elizabeth, N.J., News of March 18, 1903.*

"You may search the Bible from Genesis to Revelation, and you will not find a single line authorizing the sanctification of Sunday. The Scriptures enforce the religious observance of Saterday, a day which we never sanctify."—*James Cardinal Gibbon, The Faith of Our Fathers, chapter 8.*

"If Protestants would follow the Bible, they should worship God on the Sabbath day. In keeping the Sunday they are following a law of the Catholic Church."—*Albert Smith, Chancellor of the Archdiocese of Baltimore, replying for the Cardinal, in a letter of February 10, 1920.*

"We hold upon this earth the place of God Almighty."—*Pope Leo XIII, Encyclical Letter, June 20, 1894; The Great Encyclical Letters of Leo XIII, p. 304.*

"Prove to me from the Bible alone that I am bound to keep Sunday holy. There is no such law in the Bible. It is a law of the holy Catholic Church alone. The Bible says 'Remember the Sabbath day to keep it holy.' The Catholic Church says, No. By my divine power I abolish the Sabbath day and command you to keep holy the first day of the week. And lo! The entire civilized world bows down in reverent obedience to the command of the Holy Catholic Church."—*Priest Thomas Enright, CSSR, President of Redemptorist College, Kansas City, MO, in a lecture at Hartford, Kansas Weekly Call, February 22, 1884, and the American Sentinel, a New York Roman Catholic journal, in June 1893, p. 173.*

"Of course the Catholic Church claims that the change was her act . . AND THE ACT IS A MARK of her ecclesiastical power."—*From the office of Cardinal Gibbons, through Chan-*

cellor H. F. Thomas, November 11, 1895.

How important it is that we obey the commandments of God rather than the commandments of men.

"Know ye not, that to whom ye yield yourselves servants to obey, his servants ye are to whom ye obey?"—*Romans 6:16.*

"It is written, Thou shalt worship the Lord thy God, and Him only shalt thou serve."—*Matthew 4:10.*

"But in vain they do worship Me, teaching for doctrines the commandments of men."—*Matthew 15:9.*

"How long halt ye between two opinions? If the Lord be God, follow Him; but if Baal, then follow him."—*1 Kings 18:21.*

FACT NUMBER NINE—**The seventh-day Sabbath, instituted by God at the Creation of this world, is the seal of His governmental authority.**

God's basic governmental code for mankind is the Ten Commandments. Of those ten, only the Sabbath commandment reveals the name of our Creator and Lawgiver.

Of all the commandments in the Decalogue, only the Fourth Commandment reveals the (1) name, (2) authority, and (3) dominion of the Author of this Law:

In six days, (1) the Lord (name) (2) made (office—the Creator) (3) heaven and earth (dominion or territory over which He rules). **This commandment alone contains the seal of God.**

Examine the notary seal of a notary public or any other legal seal. Each seal will always contain the above three identifying marks.

"Remember the Sabbath day, to keep it holy . . for in six days the Lord made heaven and earth, the sea, and all that in them is, and rested the seventh day: wherefore the Lord blessed the Sabbath day, and hallowed it."—*Exodus 20:8, 11.*

The Sabbath commandment contains the seal of God, and the Sabbath itself—given in this commandment—is inseparably connected with this seal. For the Sabbath is the basis of all true worship of our Creator. And this worship lies at the heart of all our acknowledgment of His authority as our Creator and our God. The Sabbath is ever to be kept as a sign that we belong to Him. And the keeping of it brings us within the circle of this seal.

The seal is impressed in order that all may know the authority from whence it comes—and that all may know that it is not to be changed. **The seventh-day Sabbath comes from God. Let no man dare to tamper with it—for the seal of God is upon it.**

"Now, O king, establish the decree, and sign the writing, that it be not changed."—*Daniel 6:8.*

"Bind up the testimony, seal the law among My disciples."—*Isaiah 8:16.*

"It [the Sabbath] is a sign between Me and the children of Israel for ever: for in six days the Lord made heaven and earth, and on the seventh day He rested, and was refreshed."—*Exodus 31:17.*

"And hallow My Sabbaths; and they shall be a sign between Me and you, that ye may know that I am the Lord your *God."— Ezekiel 20:20.*

The Sabbath is a powerful sign of God's creative power—not only of this earth, but within our lives as well. It requires the same power to clean our lives and redeem us as it did to create us in the first place.

"Create in me a clean heart, O God."—*Psalm 51:10.*

"We are . . created in Christ Jesus unto good works."—*Ephesians 2:10.*

The Bible tells us there is to be a special sealing work in these last days, just before the return of Jesus in the clouds of heaven.

"And I saw another angel ascending from the east, having the seal of the living God: and he cried with a loud voice to the four angels . . saying, Hurt not the earth, neither the sea, or the trees, till we have sealed the servants of our God in their foreheads."—*Revelation 7:2-3 (Ezekiel 9:1-6).*

"And I looked, and, lo, a Lamb stood on the mount Sion, and with Him an hundred forty and four thousand, having His Father's name written in their foreheads."—*Revelation 14:1.*

The name of the Father is expressive of His character. When

Moses asked to see the glory of God, the Lord passed by and told His name—that which He was like:

"The Lord, the Lord God, merciful and gracious, longsuffering, and abundant in goodness and truth."—*Exodus 34:6.*

And as we look at God's holy law, we see another view of His character. It is a transcript of that character. It is God's characteristics written on everlasting stone. He wants us to live it out in our lives.

When God writes His name on your forehead and right hand, this means He writes His law on your heart. This is the work of the new covenant (Heb 8:10; 10:16; Jer 31:33); and that work reaches its climax when God "seals in" His own people, just before He returns the second time in the clouds of heaven. What are those sealed ones like? They are fully obedient to the Law of God:

"And in their mouth was found no guile: for they are without fault before the throne of God."—*Revelation 14:5.*

But in the final crisis before His return, there will be a people who will yield obedience to the beast instead of to God.

"And the third angel followed them, saying with a loud voice, If any man worship the beast and his image, and receive his mark in his forehead, or in his hand, the same shall drink of the wine of the wrath of God."—*Revelation 14:9-10.*

"And he [the beast] causeth all, both small and great, rich and poor, free and bond, to receive a mark in their right hand, or in their foreheads."—*Revelation 13:16.*

In contrast with those who serve the beast and receive his mark, are those who in the last days will serve God and receive His seal. How can they be identified? God has told us in His Word. Here is a description of God's remnant people at the end of time:

"And the dragon [Satan, working through his agents] was wroth with the woman [the true church], and went to make war with the remnant of her seed, which keep the commandments of God, and have the testimony of Jesus Christ."—*Revelation 12:17.*

And the third angel of Revelation 14, which warns men to not receive the mark of the beast, also tells them how to avoid receiving it—by keeping the commandments of God through the faith of Jesus Christ:

"And the third angel followed them, saying with a loud voice, If any man worship the beast and his image, and receive his mark in his forehead, or in his hand, the same shall drink of the wine of the wrath of God, which is poured out without mixture . . Here is the patience of the saints: here are they that keep the commandments of God, and the faith of Jesus."—*Revelation 14:9-10, 12.*

The final crisis will be caused by a decree by the beast, that all men must disobey a commandment of the law of God. The nations and churches of the world will not require men to steal or lie or commit adultery. The growing movement toward national Sunday laws is growing stronger every passing year. It is seen that in this point, and in this alone, will be found the heart of the crisis of Revelation 13 and 14.

The first angel of Revelation 14 calls on all men everywhere, today, to reverence God—by returning to the worship of the Creator of all things.

"And I saw another angel fly in the midst of heaven, having the everlasting gospel to preach unto them that dwell on the earth, and to every nation, and kindred, and tongue, and people:

"Saying with a loud voice, Fear God, and give glory to Him; for the hour of His judgment is come: and worship Him that made heaven, and earth, and the sea, and the fountains of waters."—*Revelation 14:6-7.*

As the crisis nears, we must prepare for it.

"The observance of Sunday by the Protestants is an homage they pay, in spite of themselves, to the authority of the [Catholic] Church."—*Monsignor Louis Segur, Plain Talk About the Protestantism of Today, p. 213.*

Already we are facing Sunday closing laws on local levels. Men are prohibited from doing business on the first working day of the week, lest they be fined or imprisoned. And the situation will grow worse in the days just ahead.

"That the image of the beast should both speak, and cause [decree] that as many as would not worship the image of the beast should be killed. And he causeth all, both small and great, rich and poor, free and bond, to receive a mark in their right hand, or in their foreheads: and that no man might buy or sell, save he that had the mark."—*Revelation 13:15-17.*

But there is victory for those who will stand true to the God of heaven. There is overcoming power for those who will "keep the commandments of God and the faith of Jesus" (Rev 14:12).

"And I saw . . them that had gotten the victory over the beast, and over his image, and over his mark, and over the number of his name, stand on the sea of glass, having the harps of God."— *Revelation 15:2.*

FACT NUMBER TEN—**God's remnant people will keep the Bible Sabbath, and that holy day will be kept throughout eternity.**

(1) **Even though there are over two thousand denominations today, the remnant people of God, living at the end of time, can be identified. God has identified them for us.** After speaking about how the antichrist power in the Dark Ages tried for centuries to destroy the people of God, **we are told how to identify them in these last days, just before Christ returns in the clouds for His own:**

"And the dragon was wroth with the woman, and went to make war with the remnant of her seed, which keep the commandments of God, and have the testimony of Jesus Christ."— *Revelation 12:17.*

And the third angel, after warning all men against receiving the mark of the beast, tells us clearly who will be the little group that will stand apart from this almost universal apostasy:

"Here is the patience of the saints: here are they that keep the commandments of God, and the faith of Jesus."—*Revelation 14:12.*

It will be an almost universal apostasy. All around us can be seen a rising tide of rebellion against the Ten Commandments. The colleges and universities teach that man is but an animal descended from worms and amoeba. The churches teach that God destroyed the

Ten Commandments at Calvary, and that Jesus died to take sinners to heaven just as they are. Governmental agencies are relaxing moral restrictions and permitting gambling, abortion, homosexuality, and other vices.

This world is becoming a curse, but soon God will intervene. Prophecy tells us that before the end there will be a small company who will stand true to the commandments of God, by faith in Jesus Christ.

(2) And soon this present evil world will be ended suddenly by the return of Jesus Christ—and heaven will begin for the faithful.

And in that heaven the seventh-day Sabbath will be kept forever. God's people suffered and died for it down here, and they will worship God on that holy day through all ages to come.

Revelation 21 and 22 tells us about this new life with Jesus, when sin has come to an end and the wicked are no longer alive.

"And I saw a new heaven and a new earth: for the first heaven and the first earth were passed away; and there was no more sea . . And he shewed me a pure river of water of life, clear as crystal, proceeding out of the throne of God and of the Lamb."—*Revelation 21:1; 22:1.*

And then **we are told who will enter that beautiful new world:**

"Blessed are they that do His commandments, that they may have right to the tree of life, and may enter in through the gates into the city."—*Revelation 22:14.*

But more: **There is the promise that they will keep the holy Sabbath through all eternity:**

"For, behold, I create a new heavens and a new earth: and the former shall not be remembered, nor come into mind . . And they shall build houses, and inhabit them; and they shall plant vineyards, and eat the fruit of them. They shall not build, and another inhabit; they shall not plant, and another eat: for as the days of a tree are the days of My people, and Mine elect shall long enjoy the work of their hands . . The wolf and the lamb shall feed together, and the lion shall eat straw like the bullock; and dust shall be the serpent's meat. They shall not hurt nor destroy in all My holy mountain, saith the Lord . .

"For as the new heavens and the new earth, which I will make, shall remain before Me, saith the Lord, so shall your seed and your name remain. And it shall come to pass, that from one new moon to another, and from one Sabbath to another, shall all flesh come to worship before Me, saith the Lord."—*Isaiah 65:17, 21-22, 25; 66:22-23.*

Now you have seen God's plan for His people. And it is a wonderful one. It can begin for you right now. And it will continue on throughout eternity. Why not begin today—this very week? Ask God to forgive you for the past, and tell Him that, by His grace, you will worship your Creator on His day! This is the best decision you can make. Go to Him just now. He will help you make it.

And next Sabbath—begin that holy walk with God on His day, the holy day of Isaiah 58. Read that chapter and see the blessings He will add, if you will but let Him take over your life.

But think not that there will be no problems or trials. Satan will bring many upon you. He hates the Sabbath and all who will stand loyal to it. Yet if you will determine to be true to God and His Word, you will have strength from above to go through all that lies ahead.

And one day soon, if faithful to the end, you with the redeemed of all ages will rejoice on the sea of glass and will receive from the hand of Jesus the overcomer's crown. And you will be given that new name, expressive of a new character. And you will begin a walk with Jesus that will last through all eternity to come.

"And one of the elders answered, saying unto me, What are these which are arrayed in white robes? and whence come they?

"And I said unto him, Sir, thou knowest. And he said unto me, These are they which came out of great tribulation, and have washed their robes, and made them white in the blood of the Lamb.

"Therefore are they before the throne of God, and serve Him day and night in His temple: and He that sitteth on the throne shall dwell among them.

"They shall hunger no more, neither thirst any more; neither shall the sun light on them, nor any heat.

Helpful Bible Studies

THE BIBLE: DIVINE GUIDANCE FOR YOUR LIFE

What is the purpose of the Bible?

2 Peter 1:21—"For the prophecy came not in old time by the will of man, but holy men of God spake as they were moved by the Holy Ghost."

John 20:30-31—"And many other signs truly did Jesus in the presence of His disciples, which are not written in this book: But these are written, that ye might believe that Jesus is the Christ, the Son of God; and that believing ye might have life through His name."

Psalm 119:11—"Thy Word have I hid in mine heart, that I might not sin against Thee."

Psalm 119:105—"Thy Word is a lamp unto my feet, and a light unto my path."

Romans 15:4—"For whatsoever things were written aforetime were written for our learning, that we through patience and comfort of the Scriptures might have hope."

How should we study the Bible?

Acts 17:11—"These were more noble than those in Thessalonica, in that they received the Word with all readiness of mind, and searched the Scriptures daily, whether those things were so."

Isaiah 28:10—"For precept must be upon precept, precept upon precept; line upon line, line upon line; here a little, and there a little."

2 Timothy 2:15—"Study to show thyself approved unto God, a workman that needeth not to be ashamed, rightly dividing the word of truth."

John 5:39—"Search the Scriptures, for in them ye think ye have eternal life; and they are they which testify of Me."

GOD'S PLAN TO SAVE YOU FROM SIN

Romans 3:23—"For all have sinned and come short of the glory of God."

Isaiah 59:2—"But your iniquities have separated between you and your God, and your sins have hid His face from you, that He will not hear."

Romans 6:23—"For the wages of sin is death; but the gift of God is eternal life through Jesus Christ our Lord."

2 Peter 3:9—"The Lord is not slack concerning His promise, as some men count slackness; but is longsuffering to us-ward, not willing that any should perish, but that all should come to repentance."

Exodus 34:6-7—"The Lord God, merciful and gracious, longsuffering, and abundant in goodness and truth, keeping mercy for thousands, forgiving iniquity and transgression and sin, and that will by no means clear the guilty."

John 3:16-20—"For God so loved the world, that He gave His only begotten Son, that whosoever believeth in Him should not perish, but have everlasting life. For God sent not His Son into the world to condemn the world; but that the world through Him might be saved. He that believeth on Him is not condemned: but he that believeth not is condemned already, because he hath not believed in the name of the only begotten Son of God. And this is the condemnation, that light is come into the world, and men loved darkness rather than light, because their deeds were evil. For every one that doeth evil hateth the light, neither cometh to the light, lest his deeds should be reproved."

Luke 19:10—"For the Son of man is come to seek and to save that which was lost."

Matthew 1:21—"He shall save His people from their sins."

Isaiah 53:6—"All we like sheep have gone astray; we have turned every one to his own way; and the Lord hath laid on him the iniquity of us all."

Acts 16:31—"Believe on the Lord Jesus Christ, and thou shalt be saved."

2 Corinthians 6:2—"Now is the accepted time; behold, now is the day of salvation."

John 1:12—"But as many as received Him, to them gave He power to become the sons of God, even to them that believe on His name."

Galatians 2:20—"I am crucified with Christ: nevertheless I live; yet not I, but Christ liveth in me: and the life which I now live in the flesh I live by the faith of the Son of God, who loved me, and gave Himself for me."

John 3:3—"Verily, verily, I say unto thee, Except a man be born again, he cannot see the kingdom of God."

2 Corinthians 5:17—"Therefore if any man be in Christ, he is a new creature: old things are passed away; behold, all things are become new."

Philippians 2:13—"For it is God which worketh in you both to will and to do of His good pleasure."

Hebrews 10:16—"I will put My laws into their hearts, and in their minds will I write them."

1 John 1:9—"If we confess our sins, He is faithful and just to forgive us our sins, and to cleanse us from all unrighteousness."

Philippians 4:13—"I can do all things through Christ which strengtheneth me."

OBEDIENCE BY FAITH:
HOW GOD ENABLES YOU TO OBEY HIM

I - GOD HAS A GOVERNMENT

Psalm 103:19—"The Lord hath prepared His throne in the heavens; and His kingdom ruleth over all."

2 - THERE CAN BE NO GOVERNMENT WITHOUT LAW

Romans 7:12—"The law is holy, and the commandment holy, and just, and good."

Romans 7:14—"For we know that the law is spiritual: but I am carnal, sold under sin."

Proverbs 28:9—"He that turneth away his ear from hearing the law, even his prayer shall be abomination."

3 - GOD'S LAW WAS FOR MEN IN BIBLE TIMES

Romans 3:31—"Do we then make void the law through faith? God forbid: yea, we establish the law."

James 2:10-12—"For whosoever shall keep the whole law, and yet offend in one point, he is guilty of all. For He that said, Do not commit adultery, said also Do not kill. Now if thou commit no adultery yet if thou kill, thou art become a transgressor of the law. So speak ye, and so do, as they that shall be judged by the law of liberty."

4 - GOD'S LAW IS FOR THE REMNANT IN THE LAST DAYS

Revelation 12:17—"And the dragon was wroth with the woman, and went to make war with the remnant of her seed, which keep the commandments of God, and have the testimony of Jesus Christ."

Revelation 14:12—"Here is the patience of the saints: here are they that keep the commandments of God, and the faith of Jesus" *(verses 13-15).*

5 - THERE IS GENERAL REBELLION AGAINST GOD'S LAW

Romans 8:7—"The carnal mind is enmity against God: for it is not subject to the law of God, neither indeed can be."

Psalm 119:126—"It is time for Thee, Lord, to work: for they have made void Thy law."

6 - THERE ARE PROMISES FOR THE OBEDIENT

Psalm 119:165—"Great peace have they which love Thy law: and nothing shall offend them."

Isaiah 48:18—"O that thou hadst hearkened to My commandments! then had thy peace been as a river, and thy righteousness as the waves of the sea."

7 - THE SACRIFICIAL LAWS WERE ABOLISHED AT THE CROSS (Hebrews 10:1-16)

Colossians 2:14—"Blotting out the handwriting of ordinances that was against us, which was contrary to us, and took it out of the way, nailing it to His cross."

Colossians 2:17—"Which are a shadow of things to come; but the body is of Christ."

8. WHAT DOES THE LAW DO FOR THE SINNER?

God uses the law to do for the sinner just what needs to be done. The sinner must realize that he is a sinner. The heavy hand of the law must be laid upon him, and he must be arrested in his course. Notice the following carefully:

1. It gives a knowledge of sin.

Romans 3:20—"By the law is the knowledge of sin" *(Romans 7:7).*

2. It brings guilt and condemnation.

Romans 3:19—"Now we know that what things soever the law saith, it saith to them who are under the law: that every mouth may be stopped, and all the world may become guilty before God."

3. It acts as a spiritual mirror.

James 1:23-25—"If any be a hearer of the Word, and not a doer, he is like unto a man beholding his natural face in a glass: for he beholdeth himself, and goeth his way, and straightway forgetteth what manner of man he was. But whoso looketh into the perfect law of liberty, and continueth therein, he being not a forgetful hearer, but a doer of the work, this man shall be blessed in his deed" *(James 2:9-12)*.

Without the law, the sinner is like a man who is afflicted with a deadly disease that he doesn't know he has. Paul said, "I had not known sin, but by the law" *(Romans 7:7)*.

9 - WHAT IS THE LAW UNABLE TO DO FOR THE SINNER?

The law cannot forgive. Law does not possess the power to forgive those who transgress its precepts. Only the Lawgiver can do that. Jesus died to redeem us from the curse of the law *(Galatians 3:13)*. The law cannot keep the sinner from sinning because "the carnal mind is enmity against God: for it is not subject to the law of God, neither indeed can be" *(Romans 8:7)*.

The law only shows the sinner where he needs to change; but the law, itself, cannot change him. And so let us get three facts about the law very clear.

1. It cannot forgive or justify.

Romans 3:20—"By the deeds of the law there shall no flesh be justified in His sight."

2. It cannot keep from sin or sanctify.

Galatians 3:21—"Is the law then against the promises of God? God forbid: for if there had been a law given which could have given life, verily righteousness should have been by the law."

3. It cannot cleanse or keep the heart clean *(Romans 9:3, 7-8)*.

The law is limited in its ability to do all that needs to be done for the sinner. A wound cannot be sewed up with only a needle. The thread of the gospel must do that.

10 - WHAT DOES THE GRACE OF CHRIST DO FOR THE SINNER?

When the law of God and the Spirit of God have made the sinner conscious of his sin, he will then feel his need of Christ and go to the Saviour for pardon. The publican found it so *(Luke 18:13-14)*. The woman taken in adultery felt condemned and ashamed. She needed sympathy and forgiveness, and Christ was ready to grant these to her. Then He said, "Sin no more."

If we confess and put away sin, He will forgive *(1 John 1:9)*. This is grace, or unmerited favor. This gracious love of Christ awakens love in the heart of the sinner, and he then desires to serve and obey God. Here are four elements of the saving grace of Christ:

1. It forgives and justifies.

Acts 13:38-39—"Be it known unto you therefore, men and brethren, that through this man is preached unto you the forgiveness of sins: and by Him all that believe are justified from all things, from which ye could not be justified by the law of Moses" *(Luke 18:13-14)*.

2. It saves from sin, or sanctifies.

Matthew 1:21—"She shall bring forth a son, and thou shalt call His name Jesus: for He shall save His people from their sins."

1 Corinthians 1:30—"But of Him are ye in Christ Jesus, who of God is made unto us wisdom, and righteousness, and sanctification, and redemption."

3. It inspires faith.

Ephesians 2:8-10—"By grace are ye saved through faith; and that not of yourselves: it is the gift of God: not of works, lest any man should boast. For we are His workmanship, created in Christ Jesus unto good works, which God hath before ordained that we should walk in them."

4. It brings God's power.

Romans 1:16—"I am not ashamed of the gospel of Christ: for it is the power of God unto salvation to every one that believeth; to the Jew first, and also to the Greek."

Forgiveness of sin and power over sin came through the exercise of simple faith in God's promises and a full surrender of the heart to Him.

11 - HOW DOES A SINNER SAVED BY GRACE RELATE TO THE LAW?

1. The law becomes the standard of his life.

1 John 5:3—"This is the love of God, that we keep His commandments."

2. He permits Christ to fulfill in him the righteousness of the law.

Romans 8:3-4—"God sending His own Son in the likeness of sinful flesh, and for sin, condemned sin in the flesh: that the righteousness of the law might be fulfilled in us, who walk not after the flesh, but after the Spirit."

3. Christ writes the law in his heart.

Hebrews 8:10—"This is the covenant that I will make with the house of Israel after those days, saith the Lord; I will put My laws into their mind, and write them in their hearts: and I will be to them a God, and they shall be to Me a people" *(Psalm 119:11).*

ETERNAL LIFE ONLY THROUGH CHRIST: THE ONLY WAY TO LIVE FOREVER

I - THE TRUTH ABOUT IMMORTALITY

Man is mortal: *Job 4:17*—"Shall mortal man be more just than God?"

God is immortal: *1 Tim. 1:17*—"Now unto the King eternal, immortal, invisible."

Only God has immortality: *1 Tim. 6:16*—"Who only hath immortality."

Man must seek for immortality: *Rom. 2:7*—"To them who by patient continuance in well doing seek for glory and honour and immortality, eternal life."

2 - WHO ONLY SHALL RECEIVE IMMORTALITY?

Only possible through Christ: *2 Tim. 1:10*—"Our Saviour Jesus Christ, who hath abolished death, and hath brought life and immortality to light through the gospel."

It will not be given until the Second Advent, and only to God's faithful followers: *1 Cor. 15:51-55*—". . The trumpet shall sound, and the dead shall be raised incorruptible, and we shall be changed. . . when this corruptible shall have put on incorruption, and this mortal shall have put on immortality, then shall be brought to pass the saying that is written, Death is swallowed up in victory . ."

3 - WHERE DOES MAN GO AT DEATH?

At death, a man goes to the grave and stays there: *Psalm 89:48*—"What man is he that liveth, and shall not see death? shall he deliver his soul from the hand of the grave?" *Job 30:23*—"For I know that Thou wilt bring me to death, and to the house appointed for all living." *Eccl. 3:20*—"All go unto one place; all are of the dust, and all turn to dust again."

4 - HOW MUCH DOES HE KNOW AFTER DEATH?

His thoughts cease and he knows nothing: *Eccl. 9:5*—"For the living know that they shall die: but the dead know not any thing." *Psalm 146:3-4*—"His breath goeth forth, he returneth to his earth; in that very day his thoughts perish." *Psalm 6:5*—"For in death there is no remembrance of Thee." *Job 14:21*—"His sons come to honour, and he knoweth it not; and they are brought low, but he perceiveth it not of them." *Job 17:13*—"If I wait, the grave is mine house: I have made my bed in the darkness." *Eccl. 9:10*—"Whatsoever thy hand findeth to do, do it with thy might; for there is no work, nor device, nor knowledge, nor wisdom, in the grave, whither thou goest." *Eccl. 9:6*—"Also their love, and their hatred, and their envy, is now perished."

5 - WHERE DID THE ERROR COME FROM?
The belief in natural (innate) immortality began with Satan's lie in Eden. *Genesis 2:17*—God had said, "Thou shalt surely die." But the devil said: *Gen. 3:4*—"Ye shall not surely die."

6 - DEATH IS LIKE SOUND SLEEP
There is no consciousness, for the brain is totally gone. When David is resurrected it will seem but the next instant after he died. In the Bible, death is called "sleep" 54 times. Paul said: *1 Thess. 4:13 (also 1 Cor. 15:18-20)*—"But I would not have you to be ignorant, brethren, concerning them which are asleep, that ye sorrow not." Jesus described death in very clear words: *John 11:11-14*—"Our friend Lazarus sleepeth; but I go, that I may awake him out of sleep . . Howbeit Jesus spake of his death . . Then said Jesus unto them plainly, Lazarus is dead."

7 - THE TWO MEANINGS OF "HELL" IN THE BIBLE
The first meaning is "the grave." (The Hebrew word for this is *Sheol*, and the Greek word is *hades*.) *Psalm 16:10*—"For Thou wilt not leave My soul in hell; neither wilt Thou suffer Thine Holy One to see corruption." This is a prophecy that Christ would die and rise again (Acts 2:27, 31-32). Christ went to the grave, not to hellfire!
The second meaning is "place of burning" (gehenna).

8 - WHERE DO ALL MEN GO AT DEATH?
All men go to the grave at death, that is, to *hades* or *sheol*. *Job 30:23*—"For I know that Thou wilt bring me to death, and to the house appointed for all living." *Job 17:13*—"If I wait, the grave is mine house" *Eccl. 9:2*—"What man is he that liveth, and shall not see death? shall he deliver his soul from the hand of the grave?" At death, all go to one place: *Eccl. 3:20*—"All go unto one place; all are of the

dust, and all turn to dust again." But there is hope beyond the grave! *Rev. 14:13*—"Blessed are the dead which die in the Lord." **Everyone slumbers in silence in the grave, rather than screaming in torture and agony. There is no pain in the grave.**

9 - WHEN WILL THE RIGHTEOUS COME OUT OF THE GRAVE?

God's faithful ones will come out of their graves at the Second Coming of Christ: *1 Cor. 15:52*—"For the trumpet shall sound, and the dead shall be raised incorruptible" *(also 1 Thess. 4:16-18)*. **Christ promised His faithful ones that He would one day return for them (***John 14:1-3***).**

10 - WHEN THE WICKED ARE RESURRECTED FROM THE GRAVE

Soon after the wicked are resurrected, fire will come down from God out of heaven and devour the wicked, the devil, his evil angels, death, and the grave: *(Rev. 20:10-15; 2 Pet. 2:9;)*. **This is the gehenna, the actual burning hell. It is the "second death"** *(Rev. 20:9-14)*. **The fire will occur on the surface of the earth** *(Mal. 4:1-3)*, **and then the wicked** will **be gone—and God's people will inherit the earth** *(Matt. 5:5; Psalm 37:11, 29; Isa. 65:17-25.)*. **At death, the entire person goes into the grave,—***and there is no fire in the grave!* **All this adds to the evidence that the burning hell is yet future. This fire is "eternal," for it has eternal results** *(compare Jude 7 and 2 Pet. 2:6)*. **It is "unquenchable," for it cannot be stopped till it goes out** *(compare Matt 3:12 with Jer. 3:27; 52:12-13)*. **What is the meaning of "forever and ever"? The Bible usage is "as long as it lasts" or "as long as he lives."** *(Compare 1 Samuel 1:22 with 1:28. Compare Jonah 2:6 with 1:17.)* "They shall be destroyed forever" *(Psalm 92:7)* **means that** *the results* **of that destruction will last forever. The wicked** "shall not see life" *(John 3:36)*, **instead, they will perish.** "For the wages of sin [for the wicked] is death; but the gift of God [for the redeemed] is eternal life through Jesus Christ our Lord" *(Rom. 6:23)*. **They will not only "burn"** *(katio; Rev. 19:20; 21:8)*, **but they shall be "burned up"** *(katakaio; 2 Pet. 3:10; Matt. 3:12)*. **They shall not only be "destroyed"** *(apollumi; Matt. 21:41; Mark 1:24)*, **but be "utterly destroyed"** *(exolothreuo; Acts 3:23, R.V.)*. **They shall not only be "consumed"** *(tamam; Psalm 104:35)*, **and "consume away,"** *(kalah; Psalm 37:20)*, **but be "utterly consumed"** *(apollumi in the Septuagint; Psalm 73:19).* **The wicked will be "cut off"** *(Psalm 37:37-38; 9-11; 34)*, be like "chaff," "stubble," "fat," and quickly burn into "smoke" and "ashes* (Ps. 1:4; Isa. 40:24; Ps. 37:20; Mal. 4:1-3).*

Steps Scripture Index

This index is to Steps to Christ (pp. 4-97)

Steps Topical Index

This index is to Steps to Christ (pp. 4-97)

Other Scripture Indexes

These two indexes have been combined in order to conserve space. The one in regular type indexes the Worship Bible study *(pp. 113-128)*; the one in bold indexes the Helpful Bible Studies *(pp. 129-137)*.

For More Information

GREAT CONTROVERSY—The story is traced so vividly that this volume has become one of the most widely distributed best-sellers of modern times. 736 pp.

MINISTRY OF HEALING—Health of body, healing of disease, peace of heart - through simple, natural remedies combined with trust in divine power. 360 pp.

DESIRE OF AGES—The gripping story of Christ's life, from the manger to Calvary - and how it can help your life today. 856 pp.

. . . .

Bible Treasures –

Would you like to understand your Bible better? Eternal treasures are contained within it. Simply fill out and mail the following slip. Entirely free, with no obligation.

NAME . . . .

ADDRESS . . . .

STATE . . . . ZIP . . . .

SEND TO: HARVESTIME BOOKS - ALTAMONT, TN 37301

. . . .

Bible Treasures –

Would you like to understand your Bible better? Eternal treasures are contained within it. Simply fill out and mail the following slip. Entirely free, with no obligation.

NAME . . . .

ADDRESS . . . .

STATE . . . . ZIP . . . .

SEND TO: HARVESTIME BOOKS - ALTAMONT, TN 37301

. . . .

BIBLE READINGS—180 chapters in 18 sections make this an outstanding Bible study aid. Outstanding value. Easy-to-read print size, plus 3 indexes - and all at an easy-to-buy price. 648 pp.

MARK OF THE BEAST—Part 1 explains the Mark in Daniel 7 and Revelation 12-14. Dozens of facts and statements from historical source s. Part 2 is word-for-word from the heart of *Great Controversy*. 208 pp.

YOU CAN QUIT TOBACCO—Careful step-by-step information why you must quit - and how to do it. Has helped many people. 104 pp.

For additional literature, please contact the address below,